Before the beginning of great brilliance, there must be chaos.

—Ancient Chinese Proverb

Musicals!
Directing School and Community Theatre

Robert Boland and Paul Argentini

The Scarecrow Press, Inc.
Lanham, Md., & London
1997

SCARECROW PRESS, INC.

Published in the United States of America
by Scarecrow Press, Inc.
4720 Boston Way
Lanham, Maryland 20706

British Library Cataloguing in Publication Information Available

Library of Congress Cataloging-in-Publication Data

Boland, Robert, 1925–
   Musicals! : directing school and community theatre / Robert Boland and
Paul Argentini.
     p. cm.
   Includes bibliographical references and index.
   ISBN 0–8108-3323–9 (alk. paper)
   1. Musicals—Production and direction.   I. Argentini, Paul, 1926– . II.
Title.
   MT955.B6 1997
   792.6′0233—dc21   97–1196
                                                   CIP
                                                   MN

ISBN 0-8108-3323-9 (pbk. : alk. paper)

♾ ™ The paper used in this publication meets the minimum requirements of American National Standard for Information Sciences—Permanence of Paper for Printed Library Materials, ANSI Z39.48-1984.
Manufactured in the United States of America.

To Dr. Doric Alviani, Professor of Music
from 1938 to 1979 at the University
of Massachusetts, whose teaching and
example made it all possible.
To Mary Ellen and Robert Ames for
encouragement and Tom Blalock for
support.
Special thanks to Marge Fick and Ellen
C. Shanahan, wonderful Music
Directors, and all the students from
1958 to 1988. You know who you are.

RMB

To Vera, of course.

PMA

Contents

Illustrations

Foreword

Musicals! is a marvelously complete and detailed handbook that, in my opinion as a playwright, should be in every high school and college library in the country. It is almost impossible to think of a practical question arising in the course of a production that is not anticipated and answered in these pages with great clarity, goodwill, and humor. Although the book focuses on musicals, as the most complex and glamorous of theatre projects, much of the information is equally applicable to straight plays. A copy in every drama teacher's pocket would help them all to anxiety-free dreams and be a boon to casts and audiences as well.

WILLIAM GIBSON

Preface

It is doubtful that any book can make you a great director. But this book can offer advice on organization, analysis, and decison-making that will help you become a better one. An understanding of the basic mechanics and theory behind productions is crucial for all directors.

Every production has some "art" in it. From curtain to curtain, if it is done to the best of the cast and crew's ability and makes the most of the production's resources, it can entertain, fascinate, and transport an audience for a few magic hours.

Great artists in every art—music, painting, architecture, literature—seem to have an amazing ability to communicate on a mystical, psychic level through their chosen medium. But what if your name has been pulled out of a hat to direct a show? Will you create art or stage an awkward, by-the-numbers production?

When "art" is called for, you must generate it within yourself. As a director you can train yourself to see the unseen, whether it is a vision of magnificent staging or simple insights about human behavior. The task at hand is to express what you see so that it is received with the same degree of enthusiasm by the audience. We see spectacle with our eyes; we see meaning with our hearts. Often only the smallest bit of action, a touch or a glance, or perhaps a prop, light, or sound effect heightens a moment on the stage. Watch the details then, for things you can do throughout the whole production.

Once a small-town country wedding was being hopelessly bogged down in formal ritual and endless choruses of "Ave Maria." The congregation seemed uninterested until the bride and groom started back down the aisle and the organist, who knew the couple, grandly played "When Irish Eyes Are Smiling." The bored observers burst into applause, cheers, and tears. This was a director's touch that worked.

Be aware that even the best theatre artists can falter or stumble once in a while. You hope your production will win a positive reception from the audience. But what if it doesn't work? Remember the experience, learn something from it, and move on.

First, urge yourself to constantly look beyond the obvious. Questioning is a path to improvement. If you always remember "the play's the thing," you can lead yourself to a successful production every time.

Second, expect a great deal of yourself and everyone else involved in the production, and they will respond in kind. As any bridge player knows, you must do the very best with the hand you have been dealt—in this case, actors, crew, script, stage space, and more. Adopt a get-to-work, roll-up-your-sleeves attitude, and attack the task at hand. You must develop a knack for inspiring people to demand more of themselves than they thought possible.

Last, seek out theatre everywhere you can. See it all—the good, the bad, the indifferent—and learn to tell the difference in your own work. Often you learn as much from amateur productions as from multimillion dollar spectacles. Attend not as a critic, but as a student who asks why one scene works and another doesn't. Or ask: Why does lighting affect one so deeply? What might have saved a particularly shallow, empty moment?

Theatre is contradiction. What an audience sees is an illusion. But it is based and anchored in something that is real, a "truth" that makes it greater than reality. When you seek out that truth, the audience suspends its natural disbelief and accepts your honesty.

With experience comes confidence, and confidence is what a director needs most. Project that confidence to your cast and crew and everyone will be glad to work with you. That's when you hear the best compliment of all, "What's our next show going to be?"

Acknowledgments

Our thanks and appreciation to Anne V. Speyer of Mt. Greylock Regional High School; Ralph Hammann of Pittsfield High School; Tom Blalock, Andre Speyer, and the late Warren Fowler for photo assistance; Steven Aron for modeling for photos; Vera Argentini for editing and proofreading; Jim Merilatt at Music Theatre International, Eleanore Speert at Dramatists Play Service, John B. Welch at Baker's Plays, Henry Wallengren at Samuel French, and Jeremy Nussbaum, Esquire, for source material and services; Ed Ivas for hardware and software support; Cathy Clark for administrative and technical support; and all our teachers, including those called students.

Grateful acknowledgment is made to the following for permission to reprint and quote from copyrighted material:

Two-page extract from *Guys and Dolls* by Frank Loesser, Jo Swerling, and Abe Burrows. Copyright 1951 by Jo Swerling, Abe Burrows, and Frank Loesser. All Rights Reserved. Copyright renewed. Lyrics Copyright 1949, 1950, 1951, 1955 by Frank Music Corp. Copyright renewed 1977, 1978 by Frank Music Corp. Reprinted by permission.

Extract from *Life With Father* by Howard Lindsay and Russel Crouse. Copyright 1940 by Howard Lindsay and Russel Crouse. Copyright © renewed 1967 by the Howard Lindsay Trust, Anna E. Crouse, Timothy Crouse, and Lindsay Crouse. Reprinted by permission.

Pittsburgh Post-Gazette, excerpts from drama critic Christopher Rawson's column on the Pittsburgh Civic Light Opera's Gene Kelly Awards. Copyright *Pittsburgh Post-Gazette*. Excerpted and reprinted by permission.

Samuel French, Inc., royalty and rental contracts reprinted by permission.

The Berkshire Eagle photograph by Eugene Mitchell. Copyright *The Berkshire Eagle*. Reprinted by permission.

Introduction

The Broadway musical needs little introduction. With a relatively short history behind it, this unique theatrical form has become a mainstay of theatre groups in schools, colleges, and communities throughout the world.

More than ten thousand productions of *My Fair Lady* were presented in the single year following its release for nonprofessional performance, according to Lehman Engel in his book *Getting the Show On*. The reason is obvious. Not only is the musical a delightful—even informative—vehicle for entertainment, it is a challenging and rewarding experience for the cast as well. No other theatrical form makes such extraordinary use of actors, singers, dancers, and musicians. If performing is one's goal, the musical offers almost unlimited opportunities.

While it is true that the modern musical doesn't always succeed in being significant drama, it is a significant form of theatre unto itself. The language and lyrics aren't always lofty and uplifting. The music or songs aren't as lasting as Beethoven's. But, nonetheless, musicals from any era or background delight us all.

There are excellent arguments for considering musical theatre as the only true innovation, or change, in dramatic form since the Greeks first gave us the actor Thespis (hence Thespian) some twenty-five hundred years ago. Music and dance are recorded in all drama if we correctly understand the pictographs and hieroglyphs of ancient societies. But it was not until the appearance of the so-called book-musical that we began to see the total integration of all elements of the play as one. *Showboat* (1927) made us aware of how effectively music and lyrics (Kern and Hammerstein II) could be used to develop the story of the play. By 1990 we have seen that even the technical aspects of the production—scenery, lighting, and physical scene changes—all work to complement the plot. This is especially important to the amateur or nonprofessional production in maintaining the quality of style in theatre art.

For schools, colleges, universities, and community groups, the musical is often the theatre event of the season, attracting new members and new audiences. Getting the audience there for the annual musical usually means they'll be back for other productions as well.

But the reality is that the typical nonprofessional production of *Oklahoma!, The Music Man,* or *Anything Goes* is not going to rival the complex, computer-driven, amplified technology of Broadway's multimillion dollar productions of the 1990s. Broadway productions typically exceed $5 million in budget. Nonprofessionals typically have a tiny fraction of that budget. But we believe that it is still possible to astonish and delight an audience with skill, energy, talent, and a professional attitude. With a careful, thoughtful approach, sincerity, integrity, respect for the medium, and a willingness to take the time to polish, any production can leave an audience with the feeling of a Broadway experience.

The production of a musical play requires a leader who knows what to do and how to get it done. In most amateur groups, the director fills that role. Unfortunately, more often than not, the director must also act as the producer and become involved in everything from set building to publicity. The director must play every role from captain to custodian. All of this is a formidable requirement, especially if the director holds a full-time job as well.

As we wrote this book, we envisioned the English teacher who has just been given a first-time assignment of mounting the school's annual musical show. The new director's first thought must be, "How do I mount a musical from the very first step to the last?" And, second, "Will I be able to do it?"

We hope to provide substantial answers to the first question, and offer enough encouragement to generate confidence and a positive answer to the second. We may seem to overemphasize the elementary. We simply do not want to make assumptions about answers to these valid questions: "How do I begin?" and "Then what do I do?" We do not want to offend you, however. We will provide enough guidelines to get you through the production, but we will assume that you are intelligent, brave, and creative enough to fill in the gaps without someone "holding your hand" all the way.

We have emphasized the theoretical, which we feel will help you produce a satisfactory show, if not a smash, rather than providing a moment-by-moment schedule, which probably wouldn't apply to your particular situation anyway!

This is our attempt to create something manageable, something practical, something that might guide a director through the step-by-step process of staging a musical show. Our objective is to provide an overview that will walk the novice director through one major step after another to the completion of the musical.

We have not included some more detailed information that you might want to research as your interest and time allow. For instance, in the whole scheme of things, we will consider sets, costumes, and lighting, but not how to *build* the scenery, *fabricate* the costumes, or *light* the show. We have included a listing of selected texts on these and related topics in the bibliography section. Although of course all jobs in theatre may be performed by men or women, in this text we have tended to use the pronoun "he" for convenience. "Actor" is commonly used today to refer to both men and women.

Part I
PREPARATION

Chapter 1
Is It Theatre?

By modern definitions and practice, nearly everything has become theatre—or at least theatrical! Through television and other mass media, theatrical techniques for catching an audience's attention have become quite commonplace in politics, religion, and other areas. TV commercials, political rallies, MTV, industrial promotions—all use "music theatre" features including dancers and singing actors to hawk their wares. It becomes important then to ask what the musical is all about.

In today's theatre, almost any stage production that includes music can be called a musical. In the historial view, however, the musical is a relative newcomer. Productions such as *Oklahoma!, My Fair Lady, Annie Get Your Gun,* and *Miss Saigon* are a unique development of modern theatre. These popular shows represent a distinctly American contribution to the twenty-five hundred years of dramatic form.

There was, of course, theatre long before there was a specialized form that we call drama. Any "playing out" or reciting of an event—reenacting killing a mammoth in prehistoric times or describing a spiritual experience—is certainly theatrical. It is the division or organization of information into specific structure that makes such playing drama in keeping with the form as created by the ancient Greeks.

Why, then, in this long history is musical theatre unique?

The Seamless Flow

The musical is unique because it is, or should be, a seamless, flowing marriage of music, poetry, and plot. The musical unites the talents of the lyricists, librettists, composers, choreographers, and visual artists into an integrated whole. Before *Oklahoma!,* which was first performed on March 31, 1943, this was seldom accomplished. In the best of today's music theatre every element of staging should lead to the accomplishment of the story being told. This is an important realization for any director (or author, for that matter) to understand. If your stage business or action doesn't serve the intentions of the story, it is best eliminated.

One might trace the history of the American musical from many sources. Certainly there are convincing arguments that find ancestry in revolutionary war times, Gilbert and Sullivan, or the famous nineteenth-century production *The Black Crook*. Whether one sees Jerome Kern and Oscar Hammerstein II's *Showboat* or Gershwin's *Porgy and Bess* as the beginning, music theatre is as American as apple pie. A number of excellent books have already pursued this kind of historical study and evaluation—most notably Lehman Engel's *The American Musical Theatre*. Martin Gottfried's *Broadway Musicals* uses a different, but excellent, approach that analyzes how the separate but equal artists create a musical production.

A musical is something that moves, delights, and dazzles even as it informs or entertains us. Our purpose here is to discuss what a musical performance needs and to suggest ways to achieve the goal.

The director needs to have a good understanding of all aspects of production from beginning to end to run the show. A lot depends on why a director chooses to do a production at all. A few schools have theatre personnel and courses in performing arts already in place, but this is relatively rare. More often, someone from the music or English departments volunteers for or is assigned the task of putting on the spring show. This project is sometimes undertaken for extra salary, or compensatory class assignment time. But often the director of a school production receives no compensation for two or three months of after-school or evening rehearsal time. Either way, the director must approach the production with total commitment. It will demand a great deal of physical, emotional, and intellectual energy.

With careful attention to the details outlined throughout these pages, the director must adopt a thoroughly professional approach, constantly take stock of progress, and search for ways to improve the production. Problems will arise that at first seem insurmountable. Nothing is. Every problem can become a creative event.

An ancient Chinese proverb states: "Before the beginning of great brilliance, there must be chaos." Accept this maxim, prepare your work schedule carefully, and you will be successful.

> The experienced director knows that there are more solutions than there are problems.

Coming up with solutions goes with the job of director. So does the delightful chill that races through the director, cast, and crew when the house lights dim and the overture begins. Sometimes a nonprofessional performance fails or may drag along simply because the director has been too earnest. Many directors feel they must do everything written in the typed scripts. The script may say that Curly sits on the fence. Most likely this conforms to the specific Broadway production settings and is not a direction written and required by the authors.

The scripts you receive from a publisher are usually taken from a stage manager's prompt book used to keep a long-playing production up to standard and consistent with the original director's intention. While you cannot—and *should not*—alter the words or music of the authors, you can create your own stage directions. Remember that Broadway productions have technical facilities and artistic avenues you may not have available. What the Uris or Minskoff theatres can do in five seconds with computer turntables, elevators, or projection scenery may take you five minutes, during which time you have lost your audience's attention.

When people are "captive" in a theatre, a wait of more than thirty to sixty seconds may cause the audience's attention to wander. Viewers start to worry about baby-sitters or the ride home, or they may find the delay embarrassing and wonder whether something has gone wrong. Movement from scene to scene and from dialogue to musical number ought to be as seamless and effortless as possible.

The Nature of Song

One of the clues to planning a successful musical production is to think about the essence of the show's music. In the most popular and significant musicals, from Rodgers and Hammerstein to Stephen Sondheim, a composer/lyricist's personality gives a production its unique style. How often do we give conscious effort to bringing out this musical personality in directing a show? Some shows, such as *Anything Goes,* are clearly full of bounce and pizazz. Others, such as *A Little Night Music,* exude elegance and intelligent wit. *The King and I* has a stately, majestic quality, while *Bye Bye Birdie* is peppered with crisp, bright, primary tonalities.

A director must also consider each song individually. A song is an aria, or "air." A combination of lines, phrases, and verses is repeated in such a way as to have unity without being redundant. The composer supplies a melodic line that moves the words along with the proper intonation and pronunciation. Careful thought is given to what words and letters are best sounded on what notes of the scale. Placement of the vowels and consonants has a great deal to do with successful singing. Added to this are effects of rhythm and tempo appropriate to the given song's intent. Note also how phrases, usually one to two lines long, are given emphasis in repetition and how the song's release, always related to the beginning melodic line but different enough to create emphasis and accent in thought as well as music, occurs at just the right moment.

Then, suddenly, everything comes around again, completing the idea, message, or theme being sung about.

Using this as a kind of directorial "map," a director should ask whether his choice of blocking or interpretation of a given scene leads the audience in the same way. Avoid doing arbitrary stage business unless it fulfills the sense of what you are seeking.

Directing a musical is a bit like writing a song. It needs coherence, style, relationships, meaning, and, above all, a quality or feeling of melody. Many otherwise very credible productions lack an overall rhythm that can stimulate an audience's imagination. It is very important that the transition from dialogue to song be done easily.

Why the Song?

Let's consider why we sing in a musical.

When children play in the sandbox or in the swimming pool, their excitement and sense of pleasure are so stimulated that they begin to yell, holler, squeal, and express their joy. When we go to a sporting event we all respond to a terrific end run or a last minute "save the game" basket, and we leap to our feet the moment our team hits a home run. Why do we do these things? Because we have been so vitalized, so stimulated by the accomplishments, that we have to overreach or extend normal responses. Consider, even, what people do in an argument. The intensity with which we feel something may make us yell or shout when our emotions are aroused. Singing in a musical play will usually happen because mere words are no longer adequate for the character to express his emotions. In Shakespeare's *The Taming of the Shrew* Tranio says to Lucentio: "Practice rhetoric in your common talk; Music and poesy use to quicken you." And composer Sir Andrew Lloyd Webber and lyricist Christopher Hampton of 1994's *Sunset Boulevard* refer to the song as the "moment of sublime intention." Don't treat it lightly.

At a moment of extreme joy, sadness, frustration, or fear, we must reach out for a means of expression greater than utilitarian words. So, we sing! The musical number, then, is "yelling, squealing, shouting, striking," just as dancing may physically communicate the depth of our needs or emotions. Singing is a civilized way of expressing these things. Then it stands to reason that one simply cannot start singing because the script says so. The musical number must be approached, prepared for, and attacked. The audience must be led into the moment by the "flow" of your action and dialogue. Lines preceding a song are usually particularly meaningful, and their delivery should pick up in tempo, implication, and pacing—taking cues from the musical number itself. The physical action may speed up or intensify by increasing the number of people on stage. Movement should lead into choreography. Too often, however, one gets a feeling that now somebody sings or now somebody dances because it says so in the script. Your production can be professionalized by the attention you pay to leading the audience to awareness of and pleasure in this emotional buildup. It is such pleasure that delights us.

The Joy of Talent

When you consider the millions of dollars we spend on sports, theatre, films, and books, do you ever wonder why? In the musical, entertainment is an important factor, but what is entertainment? It is *good* singing, dancing, acting, and sets, of course; but there is more to it than that. When we hear a beautiful singing voice or watch a skillful dancer, the human accomplishment makes the whole human race greater than the individuals might be. When we watch Olivier, Astaire, or Maggie Smith, our awareness that this talent is a fellow human being makes us respond with joy and delight.

Skilled and polished performances, even by amateurs, have the same power to move us with their honesty and feeling as do Tony-winning star turns. Time and again we see audiences at high school performances rise to their feet at curtain calls. These standing ovations occur not because the productions are Broadway quality, but because the shows generated as much delight and pleasure as those costing $75.00 a ticket.

So strive for a seamless, flowing, delightful performance. Avoid the laughs you might get just because the principal "dresses up" and walks onstage—don't interrupt the story and its importance as literature. Never mind the complicated piece of scenery that takes ten football players to move; don't break the audience's concentration. A good rule is that all scenery changes must be accomplished in less than one minute. In the professional theatre the limit is thirty seconds. Don't introduce local humor into your scenes. It will always diminish the credibility of your actors and production. If you don't have dancers with enough training to dance the hornpipe or the tarantella, think of something else they CAN do easily and smoothly. Your audience will be more delighted by seeing a simple dance well done than a complicated one struggled with.

The most important thing you can do for your audience, as well as your actors, is to make their everyday lives more extraordinary, more informed, and more rewarding through your effort as a director.

Chapter 2
Get a Script!

Play publishing companies, also called licensers, should be contacted right after setting the opening night date. For information, fax, phone, or write for their catalog of musical plays.

List of Licensers

Baker's Plays
100 Chauncy Street
Boston, MA 02111
Tel: (617) 482-1280
Fax: (617) 482-7613

The Dramatic Publishing Co.
311 Washington Street
P.O. Box 129
Woodstock, IL 60098
Tel: (815) 338-7170
Fax: (800) 334-5302

Dramatists Play Service, Inc.
440 Park Avenue South
New York, NY 10016
Tel: (212) 683-8960

GODSPELL Theatre Maximus
1650 Broadway - Suite 501
New York, NY 10019

Music Theatre International
545 Eighth Avenue
New York, NY 10018-4307
Tel: (212) 868-6668
Fax: (212) 643-8465

Rodgers & Hammerstein
Theatre Library
229 West 28th St., 11th Fl.
New York, NY 10001
Tel: (212) 564-4000
Fax: (212) 268-1245

Samuel French, Inc.
45 West 25th Street
New York, NY 10010-2751
Tel: (212) 206-8125
Fax: (212) 206-1429

Tams-Witmark Music Library
560 Lexington Avenue
New York, NY 10022
Tel: 1-800-221-7196
Fax: (212) 688-3232

Tracy Costumes
(Formerly Tracy Music)
86 Tide Mill Road
Hampton, NH 03848

The catalogs may include

- Title

- Creators of music, lyrics, book, libretto, or concept

- Precis of the plot

- Number of male and female characters, list of songs, type of sets needed, and choreography

- Royalty fee basis

- Rental fee basis

- Security deposit

At least six months prior to opening night, the director searches the catalogs for about two dozen possible titles. These may be presented later to a selection committee. As the list of shows is narrowed, the director should take advantage of reading, or perusing, copies of the books and scores. Generally, these may be kept for two weeks with just two-way mailing and handling charges.

The Royalty Fee

The royalty fee is paid to the licenser for the legal right to put on a musical that is protected by national or international copyright laws. This protection is simply an author's right to be paid for his creative effort. Be aware that there is no exception to payment of a royalty fee. The fact that a performance is given for a charity, benefit, or some worthy fund does not exclude it from copyright protection. If you are using another artist's material, royalties must be paid.

To ensure that a copyrighted work is not diluted or diminished in any way, no one at any time may infringe on the work by creating an adaptation. Using someone else's ideas without giving due credit or paying a royalty, or passing them off as one's own, is illegal and unethical. Photocopying, videotaping, or audio recording of works held under copyright are also against the law. There may be instances when you feel you

ORDER FORM

PLEASE READ BOTH THIS LETTER AND THE ATTACHED LICENSE VERY CAREFULLY. THIS LETTER EXPLAINS THE PROCEDURE NECESSARY FOR PRODUCING YOUR MUSICAL. NOTE THAT THIS LICENSE DOES NOT IN ANY WAY COMMIT YOU TO PRODUCE THIS MUSICAL.

Rental materials as enumerated in Paragraph 3 of the license will only be shipped **UPON RECEIPT OF FULL PAYMENT OF YOUR LICENSE FEE, RENTAL FEE AND SECURITY DEPOSIT AS DEFINED IN PARAGRAPHS 2, 3, AND 4.** Educational institutions may substitute a purchase order with each amount itemized, but we must be in receipt of the official P.O. before we can ship any rental materials. **NO MATERIALS WILL BE SENT ON PARTIAL PAYMENT.**

If you agree to the terms of the enclosed license, please send back BOTH copies signed by a representative of your organization. Rental materials will not be shipped unless we are in receipt of both items. Note that the license is based on specific statistics given us by you. If there is a discrepancy or if a change is needed, **WE MUST BE INFORMED IN WRITING. FAILURE TO INFORM US OF ANY CHANGE MAY CONSTITUTE A VIOLATION OF YOUR CONTRACT.**

Please read Paragraph 3 very carefully about what materials are part of the rental package. You may require additional rental materials for your production. If so, please fill in the order form below and enclose payment in full for the materials requested. We can not always guarantee our supply of additional rental materials. For most Samuel French Musicals, the Libretto (script) is not part of the rental package. You may purchase librettos by returning the order form below along with payment.

Some Samuel French Musicals have published piano/vocal scores that may be purchased (check catalog for specific shows). Follow the same procedure to order these scores.

You are responsible for all Shipping and Handling Fees. These Fees will be deducted from your deposit after your materials are returned to us. Rental Materials are shipped **REGULAR UPS** (Allow 5-8 Business Days). Make sure you provide us with a street address below that will accpt a UPS shipment. **UPS WILL NOT DELIVER TO A P.O. BOX.** If you would like your materials shipped faster, please check the appropriate box below. **SPECIAL SHIPMENT NOTE: ORDERS PROCESSED AFTER 1PM EST MAY NOT BE SHIPPED UNTIL THE FOLLOWING BUSINESS DAY.**

SHOW TITLE _____REF #: _____

NAME OF ORGANIZATION_____

STREET ADDRESS _____

TOWN/CITY _____STATE/ZIP_____

PURCHASED MATERIALS:

Libretto/Scripts @ $ ꞏ each   Quantity _____   Total Amount $_____

Published Vocal Scores (see catalog for price) Quantity _____   Total Amount $_____

RENTAL MATERIALS:

IN ADDITION TO [   ] or **IN ADVANCE OF** [   ] those enumerated in paragraph 3 of the license.

Piano/Conductor's Score @ $ ꞏ per month each:

quan. _____ X number of months _____ X $ ꞏ = Total Amount $_____

Vocal Chorus books @ $ ꞏ per month each:

quan. _____ X number of months _____ X $ ꞏ = Total Amount $_____

Orchestra Parts @ $ ꞏ per month each:

quan. _____ X number of months _____ X $ ꞏ = Total Amount $_____

Please list: _____

SPECIAL SHIPPING: [   ] UPS RED LABEL (Next Day)
[   ] UPS BLUE LABEL (2nd Day)

License Fee (paragraph 2)	$_____
Rental Fee (paragraph 3)	$_____
Rental Deposit (paragraph 4)	$_____
Additional Rental Materials (above)	$_____
Purchased Materials (above)	$_____
TOTAL	$_____

[over]
This form subject to revision.

Fig. 2.1. Typical royalty order form.

(5)   A. You agree that every care will be taken of your materials and that it will be used for no other purpose except as stated in Paragraph 3 hereof. Any marks made by you (and such marks shall be light and in pencil only) in said material are to be erased before the material is returned to us or we shall be entitled to charge you erasing or replacement charges. Your responsibility for these rental materials and the damage charges are outlined fully in the enclosed documentation.

B. You agree to reship the material to us (inside delivery), 45 West 25th Street, New York City 10010) by PREPAID and INSURED EXPRESS NOT LATER THAN THREE (3) DAYS AFTER THE LAST PERFORMANCE HEREUNDER. Should you fail to return the complete materials to us within said period we shall be entitled to charge a rental fee of $.   FOR EACH DAY the material is retained by you beyond the time specified.

(6)   A. When you place your order with us for the rental materials specified in Paragraph 3, you agree at that time to make payment to us of the total amount of the license fee specified in Paragraph 2 hereof, the amount of the rental charge specified in Paragraph 3 hereof, and the amount of the deposit specified in Paragraph 4 hereof.

B. If the work is not performed by you, the license fee will be returned. Samuel French, Inc. will be entitled to a rental fee of $.   per month, or any part of a month, for all materials that have been sent to you and not returned to Samuel French, Inc., in addition to shipping charges as set forth in Paragraph 4.

C. You agree that you will place with us your order for rehearsal materials and orchestral material, with the payments herein specified, so that it will reach us in sufficient time (two months prior to your opening performance date) to enable our shipment of the materials to you by a shipping service of our choice.

(7)   You agree that the name(s) of the author(s) of the book , the composer(s) and lyricist(s) of the said play shall appear in all programs you print or cause to be printed in connection with this production in type not less than 50% of the size of the title and the the names of the author(s), composer(s) and lyricist(s) shall also appear in any paid newspaper ads placed by you, and also in houseboards, window cards and similar publicity under your control.

(8)   No changes, interpolations or deletions, in the book, lyrics or music shall be made in this play for the purpose of your production hereunder.

(9)   You will furnish us two copies of the program of your production of said play hereunder.

(10)   We make no representation as to the condition, adequacy or availability of said material.

(11)   All other rights of any sorts or nature in the said play aside from these specifically granted hereunder are reserved to us, with the full right to exercise and make use of such other rights without their being considered in conflict or in competition herewith.

(12)   All copies of this agreement should be signed by an officer or duly authorized member of your organization and returned to us accompanied by payment for any sums stipulated herein which may be due and payable upon such signing. Upon receipt we shall send you a copy of this agreement with our signature and this license shall thereupon become effective.

(13)   This contract is for live staged productions only. NO OTHER RIGHTS ARE HEREBY GRANTED, INCLUDING BUT NOT LIMITED TO: TELEVISION, FILM, VIDEO CASSETTE, OR AUDIO RECORDINGS. YOU MAY NOT VIDEOTAPE YOUR PRODUCTION FOR ANY REASON WHATSOEVER.

(14)   This Agreement constitutes an offer revocable by Samuel French, Inc. at any time prior to signature by both parties and the payment fee or charge as set forth in Paragraph 2, 3, and 4 of this statement.

(15)   This Agreement shall be covered by the laws of the State of New York.

This form subject to revision.

SAMUEL FRENCH, INC.

By_____   By_____

signature and title of licensee   signature of SAMUEL FRENCH agent

Fig. 2.2. Typical royalty order form (continued).

LONDON HOLLYWOOD TORONTO

SAMUEL FRENCH, Inc.

FOUNDED 1830 *PLAY PUBLISHERS AND AUTHORS' REPRESENTATIVES* INCORPORATED 1899

45 WEST 25th STREET

NEW YORK, N.Y. 10010-2751

Phone: (212) 206-8990 **MUSICALS** FAX: (212) 206-1429

A NOTE ON RENTAL MATERIALS

PLEASE READ CAREFULLY

Care of Samuel French, Inc. rental materials are your responsibility as licensee representative. You are responsible for returning all rental materials to us in the same condition in which they are sent to you. If they appear heavily marked or damaged when you receive them, notify us immediately. YOU WILL BE LIABLE FOR ERASING CHARGES FOR MARKS NOT REPORTED TO US WITHIN 2 DAYS OF YOUR RECEIPT OF THE MATERIALS. Please instruct your musical director and/or conductor to inform all orchestra personnel of the conditions outlined below.

Your rental materials are checked twice before being packed and sent to you to make sure they are complete. Please check that the packing slip enclosed with the materials accurately reflects the materials you ordered and the materials you received. If there is any discrepancy, call us immediately. YOU WILL BE LIABLE FOR REPLACEMENT CHARGES OF ANY MATERIALS MISSING FROM YOUR ORDER THAT ARE NOT REPORTED TO US WITHIN 2 DAYS OF YOUR RECEIPT OF THEM.

Should it be necessary to mark cues or cuts, a soft lead pencil only should be used. ALL MARKS MUST BE ERASED BEFORE RETURNING THE MATERIALS TO US. You will be charged $ per hour for erasing. If any marks are made in colored pencil, ink or crayon, or if any materials are torn, mutilated, or if any pages are taped or have tape residue, you will be liable for full replacement charges.

Please make sure that any paper-clips or "post-its" that are used to mark the score by your musicians are removed before returning them to us. You will be charged the erasing charge rate for removal of these items.

A Note On Cellophane Tape
There is an increasing trend of using cellophane tape to affix changes or cuts into scores/orchestra parts. Whenever anything is taped into a score and removed, a residue of adhesive is left that causes pages to subsequently stick together, making the score or part virtually unusable for the next renter.

DO NOT LET YOUR MUSICIANS USE ANY TAPE IN RENTAL MATERIALS. YOU WILL BE CHARGED FOR THE REPLACEMENT OF ANY MATERIALS WITH TAPE RESIDUE.

REPLACEMENT CHARGES

Piano/Conductor Scores $ [double books: $]
Orchestral Parts $
Vocal Chorus Books $.

Samuel French, Inc., reserves the right to change or revise these forms and notices at any time.

Fig. 2.3. Typical rental contract.

may need an exception, for example, making a photocopy for use as a prompt book. Such exceptions must be requested in writing to the licenser.

While the director should be familiar with the royalty/rental contract (figs. 2.1, 2.2, and 2.3), the production staff also should be informed, for example, that the security deposit requires the return of undamaged, "clean" copies.

The Rental Fee

A copyright has a limited life. When the copyright protection has expired, the work becomes "public domain." It is no longer protected by copyright and is subject to appropriation by anyone. The most notable works in public domain are those of Gilbert and Sullivan. If you want to do a musical that is in public domain you don't have to pay royalties, but you must pay a rental fee to a play publishing company for use of all the printed musical material or buy all musical materials outright.

Rental fees are based mainly on usage, which is determined by several factors. One is the amount of printing involved. Another is the size, or seating capacity, of your theatre, be it auditorium, gymnasium, or ballfield. Additionally, will there be reserved seats or general admission? What is the range of ticket prices? Does the theatre include a mezzanine or balcony? Also considered are the number of paid performances. Most play publishers are willing to work with you. If your auditorium has two thousand seats, but normal attendance is eight hundred or so, that should be brought to their attention.

Experience has shown that all of these companies are as cooperative and dependable as possible, given the strict nature of copyrights on published materials. All of them will be very helpful, but they are obligated to protect the rights of the artists they represent.

Chapter 3
Making Choices

If choices are the soul of theatre, timing is the heart. The director's choices and timing generate the propelling power behind the performance.

A director's first choice is the date for the opening night performance. All scheduling is predicated on this date. Working backwards from opening night, there are two primary dates circled in red. The first is about six months from opening night. This is when preliminary work on choosing a show should start in schools and colleges. Most community theatres will schedule at least one year ahead. It may seem excessive, but the process requires time, patience, and a great deal of diplomacy.

Musical Choices

Choosing the production is the most critical step of your project. What kind of a show are you looking for? What voices or personalities do you have available? Are your student body and your audience sophisticated or experienced with trends in today's theatre? What show would make a good contrast to other drama presented and also provide an educational experience for actors, singers, dancers, and crew?

Types of Musicals

A musical is made up of three major elements: the music, or score; the lyrics to some or all of the music; and the book or libretto, which supplies the story, or plot line. There are several types of musicals, including the following:

- Musical comedy
- Musical play
- Music drama
- Operetta
- Revue
- Gilbert and Sullivan classic

Some time-honored musical comedies include

- *Anything Goes*
- *Babes in Arms*
- *Girl Crazy* (rewritten as *Crazy for You*)
- *Good News*
- *Funny Face*
- *42nd Street*
- *Hello, Dolly*

The musical play, a more carefully integrated arrangement of plot, music, and choreography, is a more recent development. Examples are

- *Oklahoma!*
- *The Sound of Music*
- *Brigadoon*
- *South Pacific*
- *West Side Story*
- *Fiddler on the Roof*
- *Les Misérables*
- *Carousel*
- *Camelot*
- *My Fair Lady*
- *A Chorus Line*
- *Cabaret*
- *Rent*
- *Evita*

Music dramas, less common, include

- *Cry The Beloved Country*
- *Street Scene*
- *The Cradle Will Rock*

Operettas, while musically beautiful, often require very lavish scenic effects and excellent voices to do them justice. Representative are

- *The Student Prince*
- *The Red Mill*
- *The Desert Song*
- *The Merry Widow*
- *Naughty Marietta*

Revues used to be "music box" productions played mainly in nightclubs or very intimate theatres. Today's revues contain the major works—thematically constructed—of most of our best stage writers and composers. Included are Stephen Sondheim; Rodgers and Hammerstein; Sheldon Harnick and Jerry Bock; and Lieber and Stoller 1995's *Smokey Joe's Cafe* featuring their rock and roll classics.

Gilbert and Sullivan's popular shows are now in public domain: there are no royalties attached, though the libretti must be purchased from reliable companies. They are often updated, but we believe that such a production loses the subtleties of Gilbert's satire on England's nineteenth-century culture. A cast misses the opportunity to learn how Darwin and philosophers Leibniz, Burke, and Ruskin affected musical theatre. Gilbert and Sullivan's most popular shows are

- *The Mikado*   • *H.M.S. Pinafore*
- *Pirates of Penzance*

For a more complete listing of possible shows we recommend Peter Filichia's book, *Let's Put on a Musical*. It includes information such as shows for primarily male casts, those for primarily female casts, those that require few sets, or those that accent choreography. Other sources are catalogs issued by play publishing companies.

Choosing a Show

The selection of a production may sometimes be done by a department head or by a committee of music and drama faculty. Perhaps you are fortunate to have a supportive, enthusiastic administration; they, too, could participate in your plans.

> It is wise to have students or potential cast members involved in the selection process.

Experience has proven that students do not like to be taken for granted. They appreciate having a say in determining a project to which they will devote their time and energy. Invariably, when directors autocratically announce the next production based on their own preferences or capabilities, disappointment and disgruntlement follow, making the task of creating a working ensemble very difficult. Low morale is destructive, especially with a lengthy and demanding rehearsal schedule in the offing. Cooperation—a lot of it—is necessary and should be cultivated.

This method has worked well in high schools, colleges, and community theatre. Do some preliminary homework by analyzing your group and your audience. Choosing a show may depend on geography as well as talent. To treat your students fairly, respectfully, and honestly, give them four or five weeks to follow through with your ideas. In community theatre this is often the most effective way to rally support and enthusiasm for the rigorous rehearsal period ahead.

You might suggest to your potential cast and crew, "I need your help in deciding on a production because there is so much excellent material available. Please suggest productions that suit our talent and our special interests." Emphasize that relevance to your age group and community interests are important. Don't hesitate to suggest the plays you have been considering.

Once this step has been taken and some interest is aroused, create a play selection committee. This committee should immediately be given scripts of shows and possibly tapes or CDs of their scores. It may be that the most expeditious way to accomplish your goal is to schedule group readings, having your music department or musical director on hand to play and sing some of the songs. This reveals possible casting choices and is also an excellent way of improving your group's acting skills. In this process, the shows suggested may be considered one by one. Comparisons may be made and helpful discussion ensues.

Videos are readily available for many of the big names of music theatre, such as *Brigadoon, My Fair Lady, Camelot,* and *The Music Man.* However, seeing videos of multimillion dollar productions made with all the polish and expertise of Hollywood does not force your students to think about the implications of a scene or its technical feasibility for your school. Direct reading is simply better education.

Soon your committee, with good guidance, can narrow the list to a manageable size of four to six possibilities. These can then be presented at the next general meeting of the committee, club, or instructional class involved. (A number of high schools are presenting teaching courses in music theatre, which is an enlightened and admirable situation.)

A reminder is in order very early along: some shows may not be available for a number of reasons. The show is currently running on the professional circuit, seen on TV only, or may not be available from the play publisher. It should be pointed out that your theatre does not have the physical or financial capability to produce "big" shows in a style familiar to a large portion of your audience. It's probably best that you not plan to present *Les Misérables* or *The Phantom of the Opera.* Not for a few years, anyway. *A Chorus Line,* now widely performed by amateurs, didn't become available until it had finished a twelve-year run on Broadway, with sister companies in Los Angeles and London, road companies, and films. In short, new shows presently appearing on Broadway, and still drawing substantial audiences, are not released to nonprofessionals.

Some shows may be turned down because they require a special type of talent not readily available. One musically beautiful production based on Edvard Grieg's music, *The Song of Norway,* absolutely requires an operatic voice. Some musicals may be rejected due to cast size, costuming, lighting effects or because a general consensus feels that the show is politically or socially dated.

Chapter 4
Planning the Production

The second primary date to be circled in red is the official start of the formal work leading to the opening night. In most regional high schools and some colleges this will be a twelve-week block of time for a typical rehearsal/production schedule. This coincides with the typical rental period, which is three months dating back from the opening or dress rehearsal of your show. Longer periods of rental are available for an extra fee that usually is very reasonable. If your school is a regional one where students must commute by bus, longer rehearsal periods may be required.

Once you've decided on a show, obtain a quotation on royalties and rental costs from the play publishing company and be sure the show is available to you. Then, before you give final approval, consider the following:

1. Do you need approval from the principal, school superintendent, or scheduling department?

2. If you have not already done so, should the music department, orchestra director, or rehearsal pianists be consulted?

3. Have you reserved the space you plan to use for the show, and do you have it for a long enough period of time to leave the sets in place during their construction?

Order Your Show

The rental company will normally request payment of fees in advance or a certified purchase order from your school or organization. Based on the royalty figures and the rental cost, you may have to sharpen your pencil to come up with a realistic budget for the show. Once you've gone to contract with a licenser, what can you expect to receive from them? Usually, the following:

- One master production script of the musical

- Full scripts for major leads (Note: Rodgers & Hammerstein almost always supply full scripts. Tams-Witmark supplies only sides. Manuscript sides contain only the lines to be spoken by characters preceded by three or four cue words. While they are difficult to work with, they force actors to listen, pay attention, and learn lines quickly.)

- Manuscript sides for supporting roles

- Choral parts for principals

- Chorus parts for twenty (the average) ensemble singers

Most publishers are willing to provide additional scripts or choral parts at an extra charge for large school organizations or a double-cast show. A double-cast show has two productions with different casts that alternate performances. Some schools require that everyone who tries out for a show be included in the performances in some capacity whether it's singing, dancing, or part of a crowd scene. It can make for a packed stage.

A method of learning musical scores has reached a new dimension through modern technology. Music Theatre International has come up with a remarkable software program called RehearScore™. The 3.5-inch floppy disk contains the entire score of a musical. It is broken down from overture to curtain call, and further separated into instruments and vocals. It can be loaded into a PC or Mac. Because the files are Musical Interface Device Independent (MIDI), they can be played on any computer equipped with a sound card. It is recommended they be manipulated through a MIDI sequencer for which software is readily available.

With a quality sequencer, the "voice," tonal quality, and volume for each part can be changed to accentuate the individual instrument or vocal you are trying to learn. Once the changes are made, the file can be recorded onto a standard cassette tape to be played any time.

Designed especially for school and community theatre, the disk may be rented along with the rental of musical scores. The process requires a great deal of time, so preparing cassette tapes should be started as early as possible. Software is available only for some shows.

Timeline

By now you should feel reasonably secure about proceeding with plans for your production. At this point many get carried away with the excitement, fun, and thrill of it all and neglect administrative details, large and small, that are vital to a smooth and satisfactory production. To avoid panic at some later stage when pressures are very great, review the following check list and timeline.

Six Months Prior to Opening Night

1. Put on your director's hat. (In Hollywood this used to be a French beret. Another symbol is the white scarf worn today by some directors to identify themselves on opening night.)

2. Set the date for the opening night performance. Determine the show's run, for example, Friday night, Saturday night, and Sunday afternoon; Friday and Saturday nights for two weekends; or four nights in a row.

3. Clear the date with the music department, choreographer, custodian, scheduling secretary, and everyone who could possibly be involved. Invariably there are unpublished class meetings, school committee meetings, and town meetings to contend with. Check the date with other theatre organizations in your town. If your group is a community theatre renting another facility for performance, reservations may have to be made at least one year in advance.

4. Publicize the organizational meeting for anyone interested in participating in the musical show. At this meeting, have everyone fill out an informational sheet that includes area of interest; commuting schedule; and other extracurricular activities, such as cheerleading or football, which may or may not create a scheduling conflict. Ask if parents or friends would be willing to contribute time and energy to the production in one area or another, such as costumes, set construction, or crew.

5. Assemble a production crew as outlined on the organizational chart (fig. 4.1) This diagram suggests the arrangement of responsibilities as practiced in professional theatre. There are union requirements and Actors Equity standards that

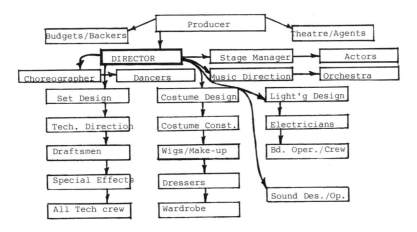

Fig. 4.1. The production organization chart.

enter into this organization of command; however, this outline can be helpful to the new director of a nonprofessional production.

Recognizing how a director can assign certain functions and knowing where to place various responsibilities for a production in process are useful. Start to recruit the following personnel:

- Stage Manager
- Assistant to the Director
- Musical Director (faculty or hired?)
- Orchestra Conductor or Instrumental Director
- Accompanist
- Choreographer (faculty, student, or hire?)
- Scenographer (set designer)
- Costume Designer/Wardrobe Mistress/Make-up Designer
- Lighting Designer
- Technical Director

- Properties Person
- Sound Technician
- Program Designer
- Publicity Person
- Poster Designer
- Box Office Manager/Personnel
- Ticket Sellers
- House Manager
- Ushers
- Parents for supplying food and as backstage assistants
- Crew for final strike

Twelve Weeks Before Opening Night

First Week

1. Have scripts and all extra necessary rehearsal parts on hand.

2. Set your rehearsal schedules. Make allowances for those with special time requirements, such as sports, clubs, and extra classes.

3. Complete the organization of your production crew, making changes as necessary.

4. Hold a preliminary meeting to discuss and set budgets with crew and designers. Set in motion the design process for sets, lights, and costumes.

5. Start the rehearsal schedule with auditions for cast, chorus, singers, and dancers. For a typical rehearsal/production schedule, see figures 4.2 and 4.3. Casting may be done in several ways that will be introduced in chapter 10.

6. Review floor plans for sets with stage manager, designers, choreographers, and music conductor(s).

7. Start your prompt book, or "bible." The process takes at least three to ten days.

Second Week (After Casting)

8. First reading: a "sing-along" to get an idea of how the show works.

9. Second reading: who does what? Hint: Record reading time.

10. Third reading: discuss theme, plot, and characterizations.

11. Fourth reading: usually for principals only. Get your cast to begin thinking as a company.

Third Week

12. Begin blocking

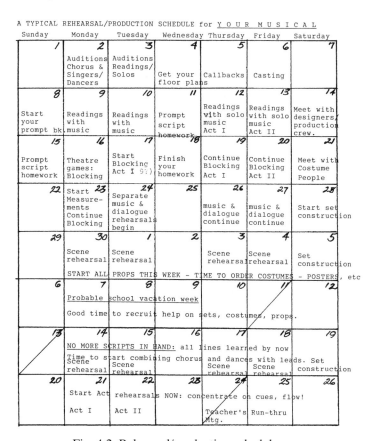

A TYPICAL REHEARSAL/PRODUCTION SCHEDULE for Y O U R   M U S I C A L

Sunday	Monday	Tuesday	Wednesday	Thursday	Friday	Saturday
1	*2* Auditions Chorus & Singers/ Dancers	*3* Auditions Readings/ Solos	*4* Get your floor plans	*5* Callbacks	*6* Casting	*7*
8 Start your prompt bk	*9* Readings with music	*10* Readings with music	*11* Prompt script homework	*12* Readings with solo music Act I	*13* Readings with solo music Act II	*14* Meet with designers, production crew.
15 Prompt script homework	*16* Theatre games: Blocking	*17* Start Blocking Act I 9?)	*18* Finish your homework	*19* Continue Blocking Act I	*20* Continue Blocking Act II	*21* Meet with Costume People
22	*23* Start Measurements Continue Blocking	*24* Separate music & dialogue rehearsals begin	*25*	*26* music & dialogue continue	*27* music & dialogue continue	*28* Start set construction
29	*30* Scene rehearsal	*1* Scene rehearsal START ALL PROPS THIS	*2* WEEK – TIME TO ORDE	*3* Scene rehearsal R COSTUMES	*4* Scene rehearsal – POSTERS,	*5* Set construction etc
6	*7* Probable Good time	*8* school vacation week to recruit	*9* help on sets, costumes, props.	*10*	*11*	*12*
13	*14* NO MORE SCRIPTS IN HAND: all lines learned by now Time to start combining chorus and dances with leads. Set Scene rehearsal	*15* Scene rehearsal	*16*	*17* Scene rehearsal	*18* Scene rehearsal construction	*19*
20	*21* Start Act Act I	*22* rehearsals Act II	*23* NOW: concentrate on	*24* cues, flow! Teacher's Mtg.	*25* Run-thru	*26*

Fig. 4.2. Rehearsal/production schedule.

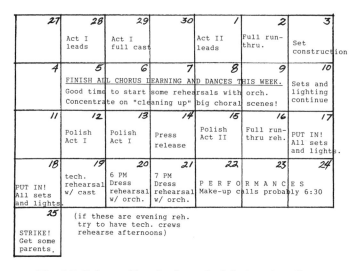

27	28	29	30	1	2	3
	Act I leads	Act I full cast		Act II leads	Full run-thru.	Set construction
4	5	6	7	8	9	10
	FINISH ALL CHORUS LEARNING AND DANCES THIS WEEK.					Sets and lighting continue
	Good time Concentrate on "cleaning up"	to start	some rehearsals with big choral	orch. scenes!		
11	12	13	14	15	16	17
	Polish Act I	Polish Act I	Press release	Polish Act II	Full run-thru reh.	PUT IN! All sets and lights.
18	19	20	21	22	23	24
PUT IN! All sets and lights.	tech. rehearsal w/ cast	6 PM Dress rehearsal w/ orch.	7 PM Dress rehearsal w/ orch.	P E R F O	R M A N C	E S Make-up calls probably 6:30
25	(if these are evening reh. try to have tech. crews rehearse afternoons)					
STRIKE! Get some parents.						

Fig. 4.3. Rehearsal/production schedule (continued).

Fourth Week

13. Get costume measurements and draw a plan for set construction.

14. Separate music and dialogue rehearsals.

Fifth Week

15. Start scene rehearsals. Time to order costumes. Start considering a program of publicity—posters, ads, programs, art work. Begin collecting/constructing all props.

Sixth Week

16. Recruit help on sets, costumes, and props (appropriate for a vacation week during the schedule).

Seventh Week

17. Hold another scene rehearsal. Combine chorus and dances with leads. All lines must be learned by now—NO MORE scripts in hand! Continue set construction.

Eighth Week

18. Start act-by-act rehearsals. Concentrate on cues and flow. Do a run-through.

Ninth Week

19. Rehearse as follows: Act I leads; Act I full cast; Act II leads; and full run-through. Continue with set construction.

Tenth Week

20. Finish learning all choruses and dances. Start some rehearsals with orchestra. Polish big choral scenes. Continue with sets and lighting.

SOUND of MUSIC

5 MAR. CHILDREN 2-5	6 MUSIC + AUDITIONS	7 READINGS	8	9 PREPARE PROMPT BOOK.	10	11
12	13 MUSIC & READING	14 MUSIC + READING	15	16 MUSIC + READING	17 ORDER aud/or	18 BACKDROPS COSTUMES
19	20 ABBESS, NUNS, LEISL, ROLF	21	22	23 MARIA, CAPT, KIDS FRAU, FRANZ	24	25 TAKE COSTUME MEASUREMENTS.
26 EASTER	27 MUSIC MARIA, CAPT. "KIDS."	28 MARIA, NUNS, CAPT, ELSA, MAX	29	30 NO KIDS ALL ACT I	31 ALL ACT I	1 APRIL
2	3 MUSIC NUNS, II MARIA CAPT. KIDS	4 MARIA, CAPT, KIDS, ROLF, ZELLER, VON SCHR.	5	6 ALL ACT II (NO KIDS)	7 ALL ACT II	8
9 MARIA, CAPT ② KIDS	10 NUNS & WOMEN LIESL, ROLF	11 ELSA, MAX, MARIA, CAPT FRANZ, FRAU.	12	13	14 MARIA, CAPT, KIDS, ROLF	15
16	17 MUSIC NUNS, ELSA, MAX	18 MARIA, CAPT. KIDS ROLF	19 PICTURES.	20 PASSOVER	21 ALL ACT I (LINES)	22
23 MARIA ② CAPT. KIDS, ROLF	24 ALL ACT I	25 ADS BEGIN	26 1ST PRESS RELEASE	27 ALL (NO KIDS) (LINES) ACT II	28 ALL RUN-THRU	29 SET CONSTRUCTION
30	1 MAY ALL·8CC ACT I	2 ACT I (NO KIDS)	3 2ND DRESS.	4 ACT II (NO KIDS)	5 ALL RUN-THRU	6 SET CONSTRUCTION
7	8 ALL ACT I	9 ALL ACT II	10 ORCH. ONLY.	11 SING THRU ORCH.	12 RUN THRU	13 FINISH BLDG. SET
14 ·MOM'S DAY SET PUT-IN	15 TECH	16 CUE TO CUE TECH	17 3RD PRESS. DRESS	18 DRESS	19 PERF ●	20 PERF ●
20 PERF ●	21	22	23	24	25	26 PERF ●	27 PERF ●

Fig. 4.4. Typical community theatre rehearsal schedule.

Eleventh Week

21. Polish Act I and Act II. Hold a full run-through rehearsal. Issue a press release. Put in all sets and lights.

Twelfth Week

22. Complete all sets and lights. Technical rehearsal with cast. If these are evening rehearsals, try to have technical crews rehearse afternoons. Two dress rehearsals with orchestra. Then, opening night and scheduled performances. The clean-up, or strike, follows the show's closing when everything is restored to order.

For a typical community theatre rehearsal schedule—this one for *The Sound of Music*—see figure 4.4.

Production Notes

- Assuming most rehearsals are two to two and one-half hours long, after school, evening, or both, break rehearsals down into Act I and Act II, or schedule scene run-throughs with the characters who appear most often together.

- Schedule some rehearsals for the music director and/or choreographer to work exclusively; it is difficult to maintain focus when elements are practiced in fragments.

- Hold production meetings at least once a week. Have each department report on progress. Problems can be solved, especially for sets and props. The meetings are called and presided over by the stage manager and should include designers, committee chairs, box office workers, publicity personnel, house manager, and anyone who may help you put on your production. If changes are being made or directors have new ideas for staging a scene with different props, this is the time for discussion and preparation.

- Schedule some rehearsals by scenes, helping to group certain characters together and preventing actors from hanging around with nothing to do. Your stage director, musical director, and choreographer may want to alternate rehearsals to provide variety.

Chapter 5
The Theatre— A Seeing Place

"The theatre," said Spanish playwright Lope de Vega, "consists of two boards and a passion."

His description aptly captures the actor's intense desire to perform and the vision of commedia dell'arte troupes with their makeshift wagons delighting audiences throughout the countrysides. Echoes of this definition are still apparent in Leoncavallo's opera *Pagliacci*. There is a great deal more than two boards in theatres today, however. The standard architecture and terminology will be defined in this chapter.

In the mid-twentieth century most schools and community theatres could not boast much more for production facilities. Newer schools, especially regional ones, may today benefit from real theatre architecture and innovative technology. The illustrative sketch (fig. 5.1) is a suggested design by author Boland for an unusual possibility being planned for Lenox Memorial High School in Lenox, Massachusetts. It combines basic elements created to accommodate orchestral events, dance, and theatre with a strong emphasis on Shakespearean productions (fig. 5.2).

The Proscenium Stage

Most school auditoriums will have some, or all, of the basic features of a standard proscenium stage as shown on the following pages. The major drawback to a typical school theatre is its inordinate width, necessary for assembly programs and graduation ceremonies. Metropolitan school stages tend to be adapted from well-proven professional theatres.

Figure 5.3 is a view of the stage as seen by the audience. A proscenium arch frames the actual stage opening and separates the stage proper from the auditorium. Proscenium stems from the Greek word *proskenion* meaning "before the facade" or in front of the *skene* or "scene house" of the Greek theatre. The Romans called it the *proscaenium,* or the "raised stage area," according to Roman playwright Plautus.

Immediately behind the proscenium arch should be a fire curtain contained in smoke "pockets" and then the main drape. This is the house curtain, sometimes called the "Grand

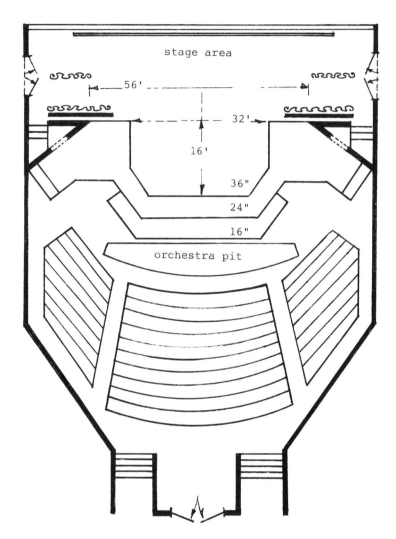

Fig. 5.1. Plan for a proposed theatre at Lenox Memorial High School, Lenox, Massachusetts.

Drape" in opera houses. The practice of opera singers appearing through the grand drape led to the term "curtain calls." Experienced stage hands call it the "rag."

Hanging horizontally across the top of the main drape is a matching curtain, or a black horizontal frame, called the teaser. One presumes the teaser was so named because it prevents the audience from seeing the mechanism of the curtain and/or the first electric, also called the light bridge. Overhead horizontal curtains, continuing in a succession above the stage, are the borders. Borders help to mask lights and, on a properly built stage, the so-called "fly space" overhead. Fly space is necessary for the hanging of painted drops or set pieces that might be raised or lowered during the production. Having a fly space for set pieces makes for rapid, efficient, and safe scene changes.

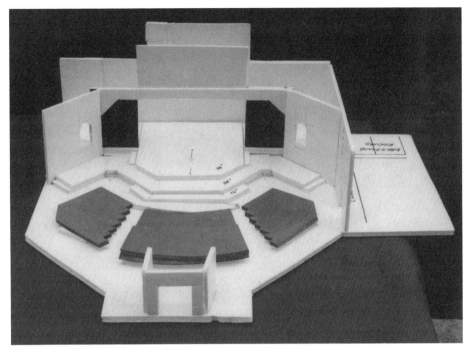

Fig. 5.2. Model for Proposed Theatre at Lenox Memorial High School.

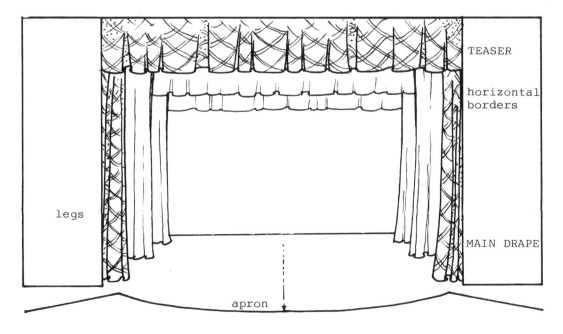

Fig. 5.3. Audience view of a stage.

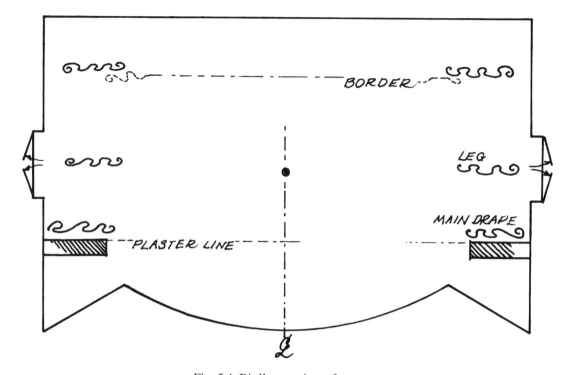

Fig. 5.4. Bird's-eye view of a stage.

Legs hang on both sides of the stage, masking the areas known as "wings." The vertical legs often meet or match the borders. Legs and borders will usually divide your stage area into thirds; thus, the spaces between them are numbered one, two, and three. The director uses these locations to instruct actors or choruses to " enter in two, or exit in three."

Large stages, professionally designed and structured, may feature additional curtains, or "flats," covered in velvet materials termed "tormentors." When present, tormentors will be positioned close to the main drape or in a downstage position.

On a line with the grand drape is the plaster line, an invisible line that separates the stage proper from the area known as the apron. At one time, the forward edge of the apron was lined with lights, which, because they were at foot level, were appropriately called footlights. Just in front of the apron is a lower area called the orchestra pit, usually reserved for the conductor and musicians. The term "orchestra" derives from the Greek *orchos,* which referred to a circular dancing area in front of the *proskene.*

A Bird's-eye View

Figure 5.4 is a view of the stage looking down from above. This bird's-eye view of the floor plan shows the stage, main drape, teaser, legs, borders, and orchestra pit.

The same view of the stage (fig. 5.5) shows the nine standard acting areas.

The Stage Plot

Left and right are as they would be for the actor standing on the stage facing the audience. With the actor standing in the center of the stage, all the area to the right of the actor would be "stage right," and all the area to the actor's left "stage left." Scripts, director's instructions, and general stage practice by designers and playwrights do not deviate from this.

The floor areas on each side of the stage behind the proscenium are called wings. The area behind the right side of the stage is the right wing; the area behind the left side of the stage is the left wing.

In both wings, going from front to rear, are specifically named backstage areas. The space between the main drape and the first legs is numbered one; between the first legs and the second legs two; and between the third legs and the back of the stage three. Actors, or a chorus, instructed to gather at "right wing two" would meet on the right wing between the first and second leg.

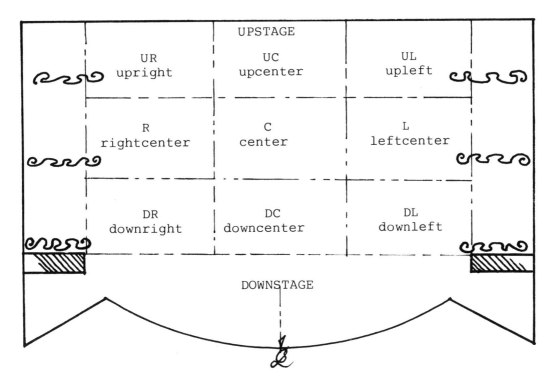

Fig. 5.5. Acting areas.

The stage itself also has an invisible, artificial line, running through its middle from front to back, called the center line. It is universally indicated by "CL" (fig. 5.6). It divides the stage into right and left sides.

When an actor on stage moves toward the orchestra pit, the direction is termed "downstage." When an actor moves away from the apron, toward the rear of the stage, the direction is termed "upstage." The concept of upstage may have arisen as early as Greek theatre, where the *skene* was raised above the level of the *orchos,* which was clearly down below. This raised area permitted principal actors to be easily seen over the "chorus," which was restricted to the *orchos.* Some later stages were actually raked for better viewing. The modern expression "upstaging" means "stealing a scene." An actor who is upstage drawing the attention of the audience away from a downstage actor, who is unaware of what is going on, thus upstages the scene. Upstaging is done deliberately in comedy scripts, by an aggressive actor, or sometimes by accident. Confusion over upstage and downstage as designations for the front and rear of the playing area may happen because one may think of "backstage" and the back of the stage as the same thing.

The center third of the stage is divided into three areas: upstage center, abbreviated as UC; center, or C; and downstage center, or DC. The right third of the stage is similarly divided into upstage right, or UR; right stage center, or RC; and downstage right, or DR. The left third of the stage is divided into UL, LC, and DL. Some directors divide the stage space into as many as fifteen acting areas. This is appropriate for drama, but may be excessive for musicals. With use, the abbreviations will become very familiar, especially when the need arises to record directed movement from one area of the stage to another, as well as to understand directions written in the script.

Most directions given to actors are from where they happen to be on the stage at the moment, such as: "Go from DR to UL above sofa." Directions are generally indicated by the course to be taken rather than the destination.

Blocking Defined

Blocking is the positioning of an actor from place to place. Blocking and movement are not the same thing and are not to be confused. Movement is usually how the blocking occurs—quickly, slowly, running, jumping.

Fig. 5.6. Center line marker.

An actor may be blocked to sit on a sofa or to run across the stage. Blocking does not refer to an actor's incidental actions, such as picking up a cup, bouncing a ball, or adjusting a hat, which are called "business."

Blocking Exercises

Blocking for a high school musical starts with the director opening his first rehearsal session with a series of exercises. The exercises will do three things:

1. They will familiarize the company, especially the actors, with the areas of the stage.

2. They will show the actors how to move on stage as well as how to sit, stand, turn, cross, advance, face three-quarters, or face front.

3. They will make the actors feel comfortable, professional, and, knowing the lingo, give them confidence.

The director should first take the stage. Then, walking about, he should delineate each area of the stage, being very specific about its designation as UC, DR, and so on. Then, gathering the actors on stage, the director may ask them, one by one, to walk to a specific area.

Next, place an object, say a chair, at stage center and ask an actor to move as you direct, indicating that a usual way to give instruction is: "I think you should walk over to the other side of the stage by going around the chair, and then come towards me so that you are opposite where you were before."

Then, start over. Explain that the same directions will be given in a clearer, more efficient manner, such as: "cross opposite to downright stage by going through up center." Type out several stage directions and ask the actors to follow them. For example: "Start UC to DR to DL to UR to DL to RC through C." They will learn this language very quickly and later be able to mark their blocking in the script very easily.

The proscenium stage is the type found in most high schools. School auditoriums are built to meet any number of uses, including assemblies, graduations, and concerts, so conditions may be less than ideal. There may be no fly-space, wings, or dressing rooms. Others may meet or exceed the features of professional theatres. Some may have other forms of theatre, such as a thrust stage, also called an open or platform stage, three-sided stage (audience sits on three sides), or arena stage. In the arena stage, "four-sided" or "black box" or "in-the-round," the audience surrounds the stage. The typical high school theatre will not have sophisticated devices, such as trap-doors in the floor, vomitoria for entrance and exit of actors, hydraulic pit lifts, turntable stages, or computerized lighting and rigging systems.

So, whether your "two boards" is a state-of-the-art theatre in a new, innovative space or an auditorium or gymnasium, so long as you plan and have the "passion" you can succeed. Using the proper terminology is a very vital part of the learning process and encourages a disciplined, professional attitude about the task at hand—your musical!

Part II
PRODUCTION

Chapter 6
The Prompt Book

The prompt book is a written record of the director's master plan for the entire show. It is comparable to what printed music is to a conductor or what a blueprint is to a builder.

No production should be considered without one.

It is the director's bible.

From the instant the house lights start to dim at the start of a production until final curtain, what takes place every moment is recorded in the prompt book. See figure 6.1 for a typical prompt book diagram.

In the professional theatre, the stage manager is usually the person who keeps the prompt book up-to-date. If, during rehearsals, the director creates special blocking or staging, the stage manager records it in the prompt book. Perhaps the director suddenly decides on the need for an unlisted prop; the stage manager—or assistant in school and community theatre productions—records it. Often during rehearsals, an actor will forget blocking and ask, "Where am I supposed to be on this line?" The answer should be in the prompt book.

On Broadway, or in summer theatre, when a replacement takes over the leading role, the actor often has only ten days to two weeks to rehearse. The stage manager, using the prompt book, prepares the new actor. So can you!

Make One

As strategic and vital as the prompt book may be, its preparation is not an imposing task. In fact, by the time the director is through with the simple mechanics, more than half the job will be done.

Preparing the ideal prompt book requires a spring binder, a copy of the libretto, blank notebook paper, glue, and a razor blade. A spring binder works best because pages go in and out easily and withstand heavy usage. A three-ring binder would require hole reinforcements so that the pages would not tear out easily. One source for

Fig. 6.1. Typical prompt book diagram.

the extra copy of the libretto is a photocopy of the director's script (after permission to duplicate has been received from the holding company). The rental companies are very understanding about the need to do this for a prompt book. They may require that the copied script be destroyed after production, but usually they ask only that the material be safeguarded against unauthorized use.

Once a copy of the script is available, separate the pages. Next, measure the size of the printed area—without the border—of a script page. Cut out a rectangle of this size in the center of a blank sheet of notebook paper for each page of the script (fig. 6.2).

Use glue to mount the script page so it shows through the "window." This allows both sides of the script page to be read—one on the right side of the book and the other

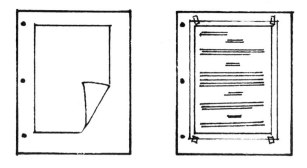

Fig. 6.2. Cut page with script.

on the left side. Do this for every page of the libretto. The prompt book now contains all the lyrics and dialogue of the show.

The Floor Plan

To make it easier to record all the blocking, the director should ask the set designer for a drawing of the floor plan of the stage where the show will be mounted (fig. 6.3). It may be simple or architectural, but close to scale and drawn to fit on notebook paper. There should be a drawing of each scene showing the stage, the limit of the scenery, furniture, doors, and other props. Two drawings of the floor plan per prompt book page is a general rule, with one to three drawings per page not unusual. The drawings should be on both sides of the paper. Enough two-sided photocopies, or computer-prepared drawings, of each floor plan scene should be made so that one can be placed between each script page for the relevant scene.

You may find a cardboard cut-out of each floor plan drawing useful for individual tracing if enough copies of this page were not photocopied. Blocking scribbled in here and there on the director's script, instead of clearly noted on floor plans, may be an impossible puzzle in the heat of rehearsal. It is not recommended.

It's possible that an extra script may not be available. In this case, the director must insert double-sided floor plans between the pages of the rental script, perhaps held in place with paper clips. Such an arrangement, obviously, needs very careful handling at all times. This method is usually required in cases where the script must be returned "clean," with

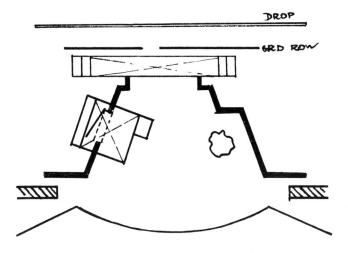

Fig. 6.3. Typical floor plan.

all notations removed, which precludes the use of colored pens. All notations on such scripts are made lightly in pencil and later erased.

Major Notations

The prompt book now stands ready for the process that will transform it from an inanimate object into a viable and priceless instrument.

> The director's first step is to read the script carefully and completely several times. This suggestion cannot be emphasized enough.

More than half of all the directions in the prompt book may now be entered. Using a highlighter, or colored pens, the director should set aside three to ten days to work exclusively on the prompt book.

The major notations in the approximate order they will be entered in the prompt book are as follows:

1. All entrances and exits

2. Direct actions

3. Warnings and cues for all

   - music
   - dancing
   - set changes
   - sound effects
   - lighting changes
   - prop business or placement

4. Beats

5. Blocking/staging

6. Indication of indirect actions

Any mandatory action is the first and easiest to indicate. It must be done because it is written in by the playwright as part of the script. The most immediate and obvious are entrances and exits of characters. Mark these in the script with a highlighter.

All the actions of a play may be labelled either direct or indirect actions. Direct actions are those that must happen because of circumstantial requirements in the script. Entrances and exits, noted above, are naturally direct actions. Examples of direct action are as follows:

- The maid faints

- A phone rings

- A voice is heard offstage

- A door opens

- A character MUST do something, such as open a window, light a cigarette, open a present, or take off a coat

- A character speaks a specific action, such as "Look at this ring, Mary!," "Let me see that photo!," or "Close that window!"

Indirect actions are those movements or reactions an actor and director may devise to illustrate a psychic moment. This will be considered in the discussion on blocking (chapter 8).

Preparing the prompt book is not as formidable a task as it seems. It does two important things: it familiarizes the director with the script, and it makes the director aware that the characters must enter and exit at certain places in the script, no matter what else they are asked to do.

Cues

A cue is a signal for a specific piece of business on or off the stage. The cue may also be given on or off the stage. Ordinarily we think of cues as signals to actors to say a line or sing a song. Set changes, lighting effects, music entrances for the orchestra, and sound effects also call for cues. At this initial stage these may be indicated in the prompt book for later rehearsals.

Warnings

Because the precise timing for the execution of cues is critical to the smooth flow of a show, cues are preceded on the prompt book page by clearly indicating in capital let ters "WARNING" or "WARN." Warnings are an indication to be prepared to respond to a cue. In performance, warnings are generally given verbally over intercom systems by the stage manager to

- The orchestra conductor
- The light board operator
- The follow spot operator
- The stage crew

- The properties crew
- The sound effects crew
- The actors

All known cues and warnings should now be entered at this stage of the prompt book. As others come up, they too should be clearly indicated. Light cues may also be entered now if the lighting and set designers are available to confer with the director.

Chapter 7
Beat the Script!

Beats are the essential structural units for crafting a play. They can be one word, several sentences, or many speeches. They are the smallest unit of the play followed by segments, French scenes (that portion of dialogue marked by the entrance or exit of one or more major characters), scenes, and acts.

Purpose of the Beat

A beat serves a specific end. A playwright naturally feeds beats into the script to generate action, much as a fireman adds coal to the firebox to drive the engine. Beats are complex, and their purposes diverse. For our purposes, we need not identify all or any of their types. The novice director should be able to satisfy the intentions of the performance by identifying when a beat occurs in the script. In time, the director may read a beat, understand its purpose and direction, and thus be able to better guide the actor.

Identifying the Beat

A beat begins, ends, or exists

- When a character enters

- When a character exits

- When there is an emotional switch

- When a new subject is introduced

- When a major shift in a scene occurs

though I were some damn criminal. I wanted him to know it, (*Turns to* c.) and as far as I'm concerned, the whole congregation can know it, too.

VINNIE. They certainly know it now.

FATHER. That suits me.

VINNIE. (*Crossing to him,* c. *Pleading*) Clare, you don't seem to understand what the church is for.

FATHER. Vinnie, if there is one place the church should leave alone, it's a man's soul. (*Crosses to* L.c.)

VINNIE. (*Moves toward him*) Clare, dear, don't you believe what it says in the Bible?

FATHER. (*Smilingly*) A man has to use his common sense about the Bible, Vinnie, if he has any! For instance, you'd be in a pretty fix if I gave all my money to the poor.

VINNIE. (*After a moment's thought*) Oh,—that's just silly. (*Crosses to* L. *of table*)

FATHER. Speaking of money—where are this month's household bills?

VINNIE. (*Turning quickly*) Now, Clare,—it isn't fair to go over the household accounts while you're hungry.

FATHER. Where are those bills, Vinnie?

VINNIE. They're downstairs on your desk. (FATHER *exits* c. to L.) Of all times! (VINNIE *sits* L. *end of bench* R.e.) (*To* CORA) It's awfully hard on a woman to love a man like Clare so much.

CORA. (*Moves down and sits on bench beside her*) Yes, men can be aggravating. Clyde gets me so provoked. We kept company for six years, but the minute he proposed, that is, from the moment I said "Yes," he began to take me for granted.

VINNIE. You have to expect that, Cora. I don't believe Clare has come right out and told me he loves me since we've been married. Of course I know he does, because I keep reminding him of it.—You have to keep reminding them, Cora. (*Door slams*)

CORA. There's Mary and Clarence. (*There is a moment's pause, then the* TWO WOMEN *look towards hall—then at each other with a knowing sort of smile.* CORA *rises, goes up to* L. *side of arch—peeks out—then faces front and says innocently*) Is that you, Mary?

MARY. (*Dashes in—very flustered*) Yes. (CLARENCE *crosses arch.*

51

Fig. 7.1. Script page from *Life With Father*. From *Life With Father*, by Howard Lindsay and Russel Crouse. Copyright © 1940 by Howard Lindsay and Russel Crouse. Copyright © renewed 1967 by the Howard Lindsay Trust, Anna E. Crouse, Timothy Crouse, and Lindsay Crouse. Reprinted by permission.

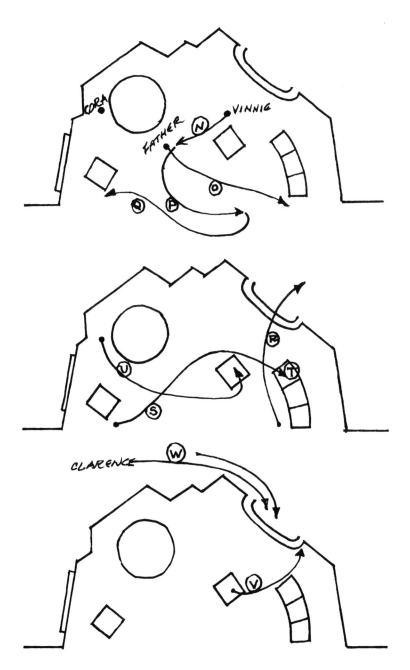

Fig. 7.2. Blocking plan of script page 51 for *Life With Father*. From *Life With Father*, by Howard Lindsay and Russel Crouse. Copyright © 1940 by Howard Lindsay and Russel Crouse. Copyright © renewed 1967 by the Howard Lindsay Trust, Anna E. Crouse, Timothy Crouse, and Lindsay Crouse. Reprinted by permission.

All of these initiate action or conflict and that's what drama is all about. Action demands movement. And movement—physical, psychological, or emotional—is the source of almost all of a director's work.

Study the Beats

By examining the beats, the director will pick up motivation and objective.

Every beat should reveal two things:

1. What a character is trying to do and

2. What the author is trying to accomplish.

Very carefully mark the beats in your script. The process will show you what your musical is all about. It will also help you understand what makes a good script. As a result, blocking will seem to flow spontaneously and naturally from the script. Notice in figure 7.1 that each beat location is indicated by a dark slash line. This helps when you start blocking because you can immediately see that emphasis is called for at this point. The beats will provide the action that makes theatre a "lively art."

If you like reading plays and are interested in this aspect of analyzing the script, we recommend studying the director's script of *The Gin Game*. It's a wonderful, warm, and funny play, and the script is an outstanding example of the director's art. Two people spend a full evening (two-plus hours) playing cards and talking. One might expect this to be completely boring to an audience. In the hands of Mike Nichols, Jessica Tandy, and Hume Cronyn, however, it is a masterpiece of theatre art. Why? Every shift in attitude, point of view, topic of conversation, or subtle power play for attention has been clearly marked for recognition. Again, consider the play's two people playing cards: how much action can there be? As you watch, you begin to realize that each shift in a chair, each deal of a card, each leaning forward or backward is marking a beat that propels the intention of *The Gin Game* with tremendous momentum and motivation.

Two examples of scripts that have beats indicated between heavy, black marks follow. The first (figs. 7.1 and 7.2) is from the play *Life With Father* by Howard Lindsay and Russel Crouse. It probably has more beats than any play of this century. More beats usually mean more action and faster pace. The constant action and quick pacing make it one of the more popular plays in American theatre history. The second (figs. 7.3 and 7.4) is from the musical *Guys and Dolls* by Frank Loesser, Jo Swerling, and Abe Burrows. It's included to emphasize the importance of marking beats in musical numbers.

Music does not stop other action while the audience listens. Everyone in the audience except the soprano's parents would fall asleep while she stood stock still

ACT   I

Scene 9

HAVANA EXTERIOR

LIGHT CUE

SKY enters from R. 1. He is carrying
SARAH in his arms and she is still
struggling. HE sets her down and it
is apparent that she is a little
tipsy.

SKY

Take it easy, slugger. It's over and you're still champ.
(SHE kisses him. She staggers after
kiss)
Are you all right?

SARAH
(Happily)
Am I all right! Ask me how do I feel ...

NUMBER: "IF I WERE A BELL"

SARAH
(Arms around him)
ASK ME NOW
(Crosses to R.)
THAT WE'RE COSY AND CLINGING
WELL, SIR, ALL I CAN SAY IS,
IF I WERE A BELL I'D BE RINGING
(Face front R. of Sky)
FROM THE MOMENT WE KISSED TONIGHT
THAT'S THE WAY I'VE JUST GOT TO BEHAVE
BOY, IF I WERE A LAMP I'D LIGHT
AND IF I WERE A BANNER I'D WAVE.
(Places her head on his shoulder,
crosses to L.)
ASK ME HOW DO I FEEL
LITTLE ME WITH MY QUIET UPBRINGING
WELL, SIR, ALL I CAN SAY IS
IF I WERE A GATE I'D BE SWINGING
(HE catches her as SHE leans to front)
AND IF I WERE A WATCH I'D START POPPING MY SPRING
OR IF I WERE A BELL I'D GO
(Swings his arms over his head)
DING, DONG, DING DONG DING.

ASK ME HOW I FEEL
(Crosses to his R, puts head on his
shoulder)
FROM THIS CHEMISTRY LESSON I'M LEARNING

SKY

Chemistry?

Fig. 7.3. Blocking beats indicated in a lyric, *Guys and Dolls*. Extract from *Guys and Dolls,* by Frank Loesser, Jo Swerling, and Abe Burrows. Copyright © 1951 by Jo Swerling, Abe Burrows, and Frank Loesser. All rights reserved. Copyright © renewed. Lyrics copyright © 1949, 1950, 1951, 1955, by Frank Music Corp. Copyright © renewed 1977, 1978, by Frank Music Corp. Reprinted by permission.

```
                              SARAH
              YES, CHEMISTRY
              WELL, SIR, ALL I CAN SAY IS,
              IF I WERE A BRIDGE I'D BE BURNING
              YES,        ◄
                            (She backs him up to L)
              I KNEW MY MORALE WOULD CRACK
                            (Crosses, backs him up t  L. 4 steps)
              FROM THE WONDERFUL WAY YOU LOOKED, BOY IF I WERE A DUCK
                                    I'D QUACK
              OR IF I WERE A GOOSE I'D BE COOKED
                        (She falls on his chest) ▼

              ASK ME HOW DO I FEEL ◄
                        (HE straightens her up)
              ASK ME NOW THAT WE'RE FONDLY CARESSING
              PAL, IF I WERE A SALAD
              I KNOW I'D BE SPLASHING MY DRESSING
                        (Puts hand down his face) ▼
              ASK ME NOW TO DESCRIBE
              THIS WHOLE BEAUTIFUL THING
              WELL, IF I WERE A BELL ◄
                        (Crosses to his L.)
              I'D GO
              DING, DONG, DING DONG DING.
                        (She falls into his arms at end of
                        number) ▼
                              SARAH
              Havana is so wonderful.  Why don't we stay here for a few
              days so we can see how wonderful it's really like.

                              SKY
                        (Takes a moment)
              I think we'd better hurry if we want to catch the plane back
              to New York.

                              SARAH
              I don't want to go back to New York.

                              SKY
              I'm taking you back!

                              SARAH
              You're no gentleman.

                              SKY
              Look, a doll like you shouldn't be mixed up with a guy like
              me.  It's no good.  I'm no good.

                        (SARAH puts arms around him: HE
                        pushes her away)

              You know why I took you to Havana?  I made a bet!  That's
              how you met me in the first place.  I made a bet.
```

proclaiming her burning desire to marry the boy next door. We care what happens next if a pursuit takes place on stage, and we also care how it turns out. Take note of the stage directions that go with each marked beat in figures 7.3 and 7.4.

To this point, working the prompt book has been a fundamental and regular procedure. The next step calls for all of the director's creative processes to be very active. It involves working subjectively and deciding on appropriate action for both the libretto and the musical staging. The director must establish the foundation for interpretation and point of view.

There is a school of thought that believes that marking the beats is not necessary, that the process may be skipped without losing a thing. By definition, each beat is a small dramatic situation in its own right. It is part of a larger scene context and should be recognized as such.

Chapter 8
Blocking and Motivation

The director must make the intangibles concrete for the audience. The most valuable skills for accomplishing this task are imagination, keen observation, and aesthetic sensibility. A detailed, notated process begins of giving visual meaning to thoughts and emotions that the playwright has indicated in his dialogue and dramatic structure. The end product is what we call indirect action.

Indirect Actions

Indirect actions are always psychic. They involve sub-text and a character's motivation in a given circumstance. They are internalizations not written in the script but are evident "between the lines" in a character's objectives. Because they are not spelled out, a director's interpretation of indirect action is subjective—what the director sees in a character's motivations and feelings. This points up the vital chain:

- Direct actions lead to beats.

- Beats are identified to indicate indirect action.

- Indirect actions are the foundation for blocking.

- Blocking is the director's craft skillfully at work.

An actor says lines designed to achieve a definite goal—his objectives. Sometimes the lines seem natural, and sometimes they don't. It's often more challenging to act in a musical than in a more naturalistic play because the musical is more condensed.

The typical naturalistic play has more time to develop subtle nuances in longer periods of dialogue than a musical does. And it is very important to be aware that much of a character's development lies in the songs and musical motives supplied by the lyricist. Recently, *Carousel* was revived in a new and brilliant production under Nicholas Hytner's direction. Hytner brought an entirely new meaning to the play by developing and illuminating the leading roles through their musical interpretations, which, in effect, had been previously unexplored in Broadway productions. Hytner selected actors who could also sing instead of great singing voices. He was thus able to intensify the more malevolent moods of Molnar's original play.

Even in the best of musicals, however, life on the stage is artificial. In real life we simply don't stop what we're doing and break into song and dance. We don't run into a diner and to the tune of Beethoven's Fifth Symphony (fig. 8.1) sing out an order. We don't dance when docking a boat, playing baseball, or during a rumble in a gang fight. Yet, all speech is basically musical and rhythmic, and vocal inflections convey our emotions. And we need to burst into song and dance in the musical!

The director and actor work for the suspension of disbelief. The audience goes along with the idea that Billy does die in *Carousel,* knowing the actor will live to do the role another time. In *Man of La Mancha* Dulcinea is beaten up by the muleteers, but no one in the audience will run out to call for help. The process of making the events on stage believable and acceptable starts with motivation.

Motivation means inducement, an incentive that prompts a person to act in a certain way. It is why we do what we do. In the theatre its interpretation is through action. A character must convey feelings and intentions:

1. On a stage,

2. In a determined amount of time, and

3. For a specific goal.

The director helps the actor accomplish this through blocking.

What Is Blocking?

Blocking is the placement or action of a character on stage that emphasizes or precipitates the pace, action, or excitement of a scene, song, or dance. Blocking encourages

Fig. 8.1. "I'll Have Some Toast! And Coffee, Too!"

the illusion of reality. The actors on stage are supposed to look as if they are real people doing real things.

There is controversy concerning the theory of blocking—how much should and should not be done? One method permits the director to decide what should work and to instruct the actors. Using another method, extemporaneous rehearsing, the actors are allowed to gradually give action to their own scenes. The more classic method of a director blocking ahead helps young actors and nonprofessionals develop acting technique and speeds the rehearsal process. Even in repertory style-extemporaneous rehearsing, the individual actor may not be aware of another character's motivation or objective. Especially for new directors, traditional methods are recommended first.

Is blocking in a prompt book professional? You can be sure it is. The legendary George Abbott once instructed an actor to "cross from stage right to stage left on your line." The actor paused and said, "But what's my motivation?" Abbott instantly replied, "Your paycheck, Sir! Your paycheck!"

Pre-blocking

In high school and community productions the more the director pre-blocks the show, the more quickly there will be the sense of a flowing, successful production.

The primary reason a beginning director should pre-block is that there is so much going on, so much to explain, so much to learn, and so much to decide that removing this major source of confusion keeps rehearsals fresh and businesslike. The actors will appreciate the air of professionalism that arises from feeling that they know exactly what they are doing.

Blocking

Tales are told of early twentieth century directors who actually moved tiny dolls (or clothespins) around a miniature set model, experimenting with visual arrangements. In the mid-nineteenth century the Duke of Saxe-Meiningen rehearsed his actors in full costume with complete sets for several months to achieve results that satisfied him. Computer programs exist today with which the practicing director may move actors on-screen to visualize desired arrangements. One still needs to concentrate on *reasons* for blocking.

Blocking saves precious rehearsal time, and allows everyone to concentrate on achieving a polished production.

The director may create what he thinks is an effective piece of stage business in his study only to learn that it does not hold up when the actors actually do it. Should this happen, look at it positively: it is part of the discriminatory process that must come with the fine art of directing.

> Blocking can and may be changed.

Over-blocking

Take caution: don't over-block! For example, don't block the exact number of steps an actor needs to take. Even though George Bernard Shaw often was specific about putting such things in his scripts, it is wiser to leave the actor room to develop.

As the director comes to understand his true and complete role, the moment will arrive when there must be enough confidence NOT to block. This may occur when the director feels that an actor seems creative, inspired, or experienced enough to "do his own thing." The director may say, "I'm not blocking this particular action because I want you to work it out with whatever motivates you."

The Inner Meaning

The single, most important aspect of blocking is that it must, in every instance, serve to develop the inner meaning of the play. As in chess, there should be no unnecessary moves, especially those made "just to make a move." Arbitrary moving around, aimless pacing about, or frantic movement that is not created to heighten our sense of the story and character relationships are not good theatre.

Ten Fundamental Stage Actions

The most useful blocking resources for the novice director are dramatic ideas that have been used quite universally for a number of years. These are listed by Milton Smith in *Play Production*. They are effective ways to analyze dialogue and motivate blocking. Professor Smith, formerly of Columbia University, suggests that the practice of blocking can be understood and guided by seeking out these common, underlying motivations in all dramatic dialogue. He focuses on five: opposition, intervention, change of mind, enmeshing, and pounding.

Professor Smith says that these five terms imply the basic situations that occur in dramatic dialogue. He further proposes that each of these will prompt the imaginative director to discover hundreds of usages without being repetitive in visual staging. He does not delve into the opposites of these actions, but we do so here.

1. Opposition implies confrontation: to face, examine, analyze. Its alter-ego is avoidance, "defrontation," escape, getting away from.

2. Intervention suggests intercession, mediation, modification. Its reverse is keeping hands off, departure, statis.

3. Change of mind or agreement demonstrates acceptance, alliance, support. Its alternative is disagreement, deviation, challenge.

4. Enmeshing involves integrating, surrounding as in an entanglement, joining together. Its contrasting action is disengagement, release, escape.

5. Pounding, the most dramatic blocking device, indicates a quick striking at, hammering, hitting (both verbal and physical). Its opposite is recoil, fear, apprehension.

With some careful study and observation you will see that everyday movements and physical actions accurately reflect these moods and emotions. We also see these attitudes in the behavior of animals. Domestic cats, protecting their territory, confront outsiders; the invading cat usually decides to change its mind.

Here are some examples that apply these terms to a script.

Confrontation-Avoidance

When someone walks up to another person and asks, "Can you direct me to the police station?" it is a confrontation (fig. 8.2). A person confronting another seeks some direct response from another person. He or she may have decided to address some situation face to face to resolve it.

Confrontational statements, always direct in nature, may vary incredibly:

Fig. 8.2. Confrontation action.

- "I love you!"

- "Let me tell you what I think of that idea!"

- "Okay, so what's on your mind?"

- "Speak up, let's face this thing!"

In real life, a person would find it very easy to imagine how one would make any of these statements. To confront means to stand or come in front of, to show defiance. On the stage, the director, finding a confrontational line of dialogue, directs the actor (A) to walk to, or toward, the other character (B) being addressed as he speaks the line. Figure 8.2 shows how it would appear in the prompt book.

Now, let us suppose that the character being spoken to (B) wants to avoid the issue and doesn't want to respond to (A). He might show this by immediately moving away from the confrontation, as indicated in the diagram above (fig. 8.3). This movement is opposition or avoidance, which means to be against or to be opposite in view, opinion, or action. "Defrontation" was coined by a theatre student to aptly describe the opposite of confrontation.

Intervention-Hands-off

Intervention means to come between. An intervention is implied in any line of dialogue where the speaking character intrudes in whatever is going on in the scene.

A classic line of intervention occurs in Thurber's *The Male Animal* in Act I, Scene 3. Ellen, the hostess at a cocktail party for college alumni, sees two men isolating themselves while reminiscing. Her line: "Look you two, break it up and say hello to people." This is clearly an intervention line calling for her movement between Joe and Ed (C). See figure 8.4 for how it would be recorded in the prompt book.

To illustrate a hands-off attitude, imagine someone walked to Ellen and said, "As hostess, don't you think you should break up Joe and Ed?" Ellen's reply might have been (B) "Not me! Those two are just impossible!" (C). Ellen's objective here is to get away from the situation. This action is diagrammed in figure 8.5.

Fig. 8.3. Avoidance action.

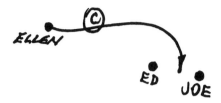

Fig. 8.4. Intervention action.

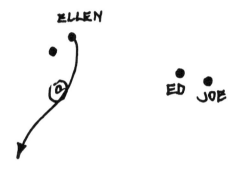

Fig. 8.5. Hands-off action.

Agreement-Disagreement

Agreement is apparent when a character has just experienced emotions but then re-verses the thought. The action should align with the new attitude, the new objective. If the line of dialogue indicates that the character now wishes to agree with other people or other emotions, it can be symbolically illustrated to the audience by having the character move to the other, formerly opposing side. Meaningful movement reinforces the intent of the scene. Juliet desperately wants to be with Romeo, even though she knows the families are feuding. Follow the blocking of Juliet's imaginary dialogue (below) in the prompt script (fig. 8.6):

Juliet

[(A) going to her father]
Oh! Father, you cannot know how much I love him.

[(B) going to her mother]
I care not that his name be Capulet or Montague . . .

[(C) going to Romeo]
Henceforth I shall be whatever name he shall desire.

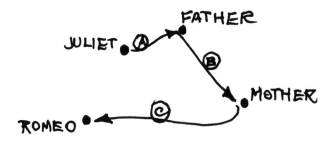

Fig. 8.6. Change of mind and agreement action.

Integrating-Disengagement

The fourth fundamental type of dialogue that motivates movement and establishes objectives is integrating (versus disengaging). When people wish to demonstrate their acceptance of someone they have just met, or someone that they like, they put their arms around them and embrace them. That action is also called enmeshing, although the term can also describe a negative surrounding. This occurs when a character decides to harass another who is different or vulnerable. It makes for an emotionally distressing scene, offering feelings of threats, intimidation, and vicious tormenting. The threatened character disengages, or escapes, from the unwanted attention. In *Carousel,* Billy is enmeshed by the police and townspeople when he cries out, "You won't take me alive!" The threat of capture by authorities is greater than his love of life at this point, and to escape the enmeshing he runs to the dock and then jumps off (see fig. 8.7).

In *Brigadoon,* Harry Beaton finds that another escape from intimidation and intolerable surroundings is necessary and says, "I'm leavin' Brigadoon, t'is the end of all of us!" His exit is recorded in figure 8.8.

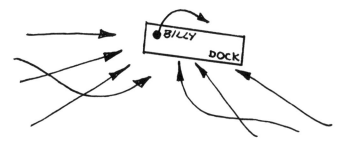

Fig. 8.7. Escape action.

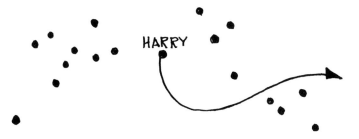

Fig. 8.8. Disengagement action.

Pounding-Recoil

The last of the fundamental motivations listed for blocking a scene is pounding. This is the most dramatic of actions, often the climax of a scene. Surprisingly, it's the least used. It cannot be used too frequently, possibly because of its intense dramatic nature. The action of pounding is implicit in its verbal usage: to pound on a door, to pound in a nail, to have a pounding headache.

Imagine a character who is emotionally bound to a chair in the middle of the stage. The character could be a teenager being reprimanded by his father; the wife being driven mad by an evil husband in *Gaslight;* or the child who must finish breakfast. The objective, not the type of play or the tragic or comic nature of the scene, is key.

In pounding scenes, the lines themselves are exciting, but that doesn't exclude other action. The director must continue to make the playwright's intentions very clear. The movement is much like a boxers in a fight, gliding in to strike a blow, retreating, then looking for another opening. This may be indicated by the aggressor coming in from behind, pursuing the other actor around the stage, or trying to make several points.

The following pounding scene is blocked (the letters in parentheses corresponding to the letters in circles on the prompt book pages) in figure 8.9.

FATHER

(To Jimmy-confrontational)
Jimmy, sit down, we need to talk!
(Points)

JIMMY

(A) (Wanting to escape)
But Dad, I have to be at football practice at five.

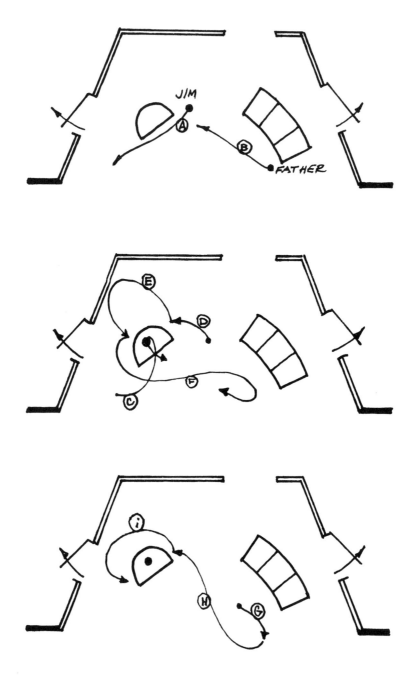

Fig. 8.9. Pounding action.

FATHER

(B) (Advancing)
There will not be any football practice if you don't sit down.

JIMMY

(C) (Change of mind)
Okay, what's up?
(Sits)

FATHER

(D) (To him)
Jimmy, did you take the car last night?
(Jim nods)
(E) Didn't I tell you the car was off limits until you mowed the lawn? (F) But you didn't mow the lawn, did you? You went swimming, right?
(Jim starts to rise to explain)
Sit down, young man, until I'm finished talking! . . . (G) Now, where was I? . . . Oh! Yes! the car. (H) Do you realize that I couldn't go to work today because the car . . .
(I) the one you were not supposed to use—was out of gas?

Combinations

Combining the ten featured motivations with physical demonstrations of the actor's subtext or objectives allows the director to illustrate what the audience must know as the play progresses. The director must work to develop a universal eye, one that sees every movement on stage, especially those conveying an actor's subtext or objectives, through the eyes of the audience. The director's constant question should be "What reaction will the audience have to that?"

Weight of Stage Areas

Blocking should also consider the attention-getting implications of the stage area. Generally, center stage takes more attention for itself, whereas stage left has the least tension and stage right the most anticipation. Since most people read written words from left to right, the stage right side seems more attention-getting than the left. Most people are right-handed. Opposition to right-handedness creates more tension. Movement from left to right feels more positive and more dramatic than from right to left.

Movement from one side to the other, maintaining the same distance from the audience, is passive. It's static and boring (see fig. 8.10).

Movement forward or backward toward the audience dominates the picture plane and forces the audience to watch the actor (fig. 8.11). Think of the expression "Come to the point!"

Movement on any diagonal or series of diagonals may suggest vitality and action. It may also be used to suggest confusion or chaos (fig. 8.12). As the song lyric says, "jumpy as a puppet on a string. . . . "

Sweeping or circular movements (fig. 8.13) are rhythmic, grand, feminine, graceful, very musical. They can also be used to suggest avoiding something. Think of the expression "Beating around the bush."

An example of combined patterns of movement is shown in figure 8.14.

To assist in blocking watch the movements of the actor's entire body. When an actor delivers rapid, emotionally charged dialogue while standing stiffly or moving slowly across the stage, movement conflicts with meaning. The actor may have learned all the lines but not the meaning of the words. Help him match the action to the words.

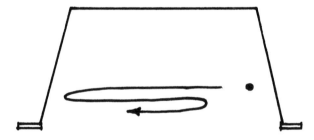

Fig. 8.10. Passive movement side-to-side.

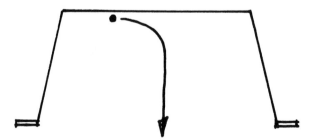

Fig. 8.11. Commanding forward movement.

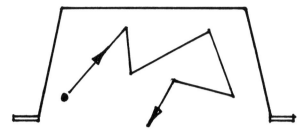

Fig. 8.12. Active diagonal movement.

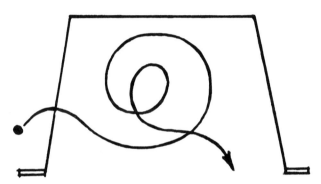

Fig. 8.13. A rhythmic curvilinear movement.

Go to the rescue with motivation. If an actor is motivated by his lines and his objectives, he will be able to avoid shuffling.

Blocking Examples

To get a feel for reading blocking diagrams, review figures 8.15 and 8.16.

In the drawing of a prepared prompt script, the mounted script is on the left side of the book, and the printed floor plan is opposite on the right side. With the prompt book opened flat, what and when something is supposed to happen is right before the director's eyes.

Actions by actors are given successive letters on every page—A, B, C, and so on. Should the twenty-six letters be used up and more needed, start again at the beginning of the alphabet. The letter on the script page corresponds exactly to the letter on the floor plan facing it, diagramming when the actors move and where they go.

To illustrate, we read on the script page (fig. 8.15) that the character Mary crosses to center at A. On the floor plan page opposite (fig. 8.16), at A we can see exactly where Mary enters at right wing two and where she stops on the raised level at center stage.

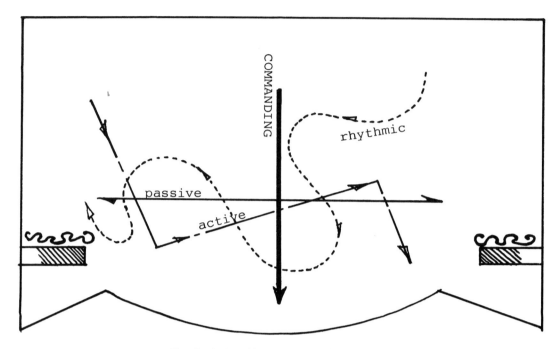

Fig. 8.14. Combined patterns of movement.

There is some intervening stage business, and then it is noted on the script that she crosses to the bench at B and sits at the X. This corresponds to the path marked B on the floor plan. In the script, midway through Steve's lines is the letter C, which reads that he crosses to Mary. On the floor plan, C starts at downstage right and crosses upstage through center stage to where Mary was standing before she sat down.

Next, the orchestra is warned about its upcoming cue, and Mary crosses downstage left and sings. The floor plan shows where she left the bench and the position she takes far downstage to sing (D). During the song, she returns to Steve, as indicated in the lower floor plan, at E. At F she circles around him; and at G she crosses center stage to go far downstage right where she presents herself to the audience. In the meantime, Steve is instructed to sit. The floor plan indicates their positions at blackout when Mary exits to the right and Steve goes off to the left (H).

Also on the script page are warnings to the orchestra conductor and lighting technicians to stand by for their cues as well as a warning to the stage technicians that a scene change is coming up.

Another example from a prompt book (figs. 8.17 and 8.18) shows the method used to diagram a musical number. So much is going on that it would seem to be complicated to record, but there is an easy technique that may be followed.

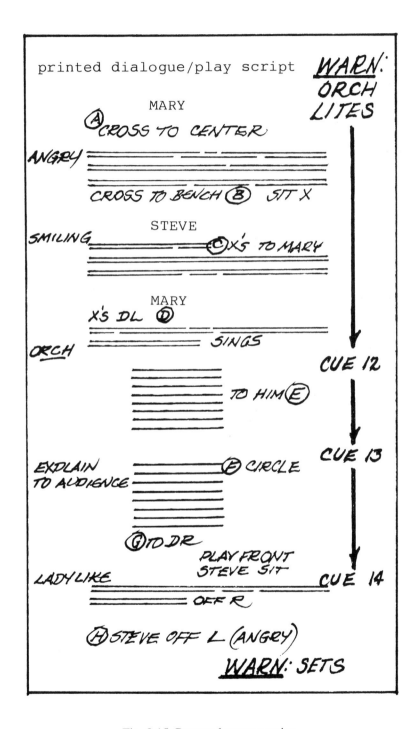

Fig. 8.15. Prepared prompt script.

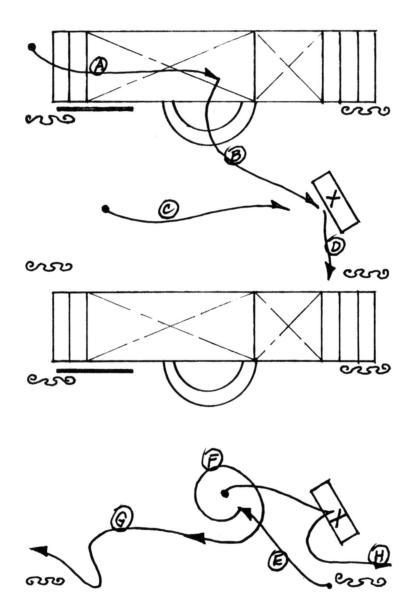

Fig. 8.16. Prepared prompt script.

At the very top of the script page we can see that a warning must be given to the board operator that the lights will dim on the chorus and that a spot will "pick up," or come up, on Mary. Then at A we read that the chorus enters upstage from the left and right wings in three; they come down the stairs, with each side crossing at stage center to go down stage left and down stage right. This movement is diagrammed on the floor plan. During the second chorus of the music, the chorus has separated with three members on each side, and at B the three members on each side cross back up to the level where Mary enters upstage center and stands. At C the chorus kneels, and, as the lights dim on the chorus, a spot picks up Mary. On D the back row of the chorus rises; on E the front row rises; and on F the chorus on both levels exits stage right and stage left while Mary crosses to downstage center on the applause (G).

One point needs emphasis. The prompt book does not have to be done all at once. Doing one or two scenes at a time initiates a fresh viewpoint. It also allows the director to think about how to rehearse a scene or consider aspects of interpretation.

A prompt book prepared, page by page, in the foregoing manner offers multifold benefits:

- It provides a thoughtful, creative record of the meaning of the play and its music;

- It enables the director to concentrate on the production's final effect;

- It is the final authority during reheasal, eliminating guesswork or memory;

- It saves the director from reinventing a particular bit of stage business;

- It saves time in breaking in a replacement during rehearsal; and

- It enable understudies to learn their parts and give and receive cues without confusion.

In the professional theatre the prompt book is held by the stage manager. Alongside the director, the stage manager may assist in preparation, note any and all changes, and, once set, see that there is no deviation from its instructions. The stage manager uses the prompt book to run the show night after night, sometimes for years on end. Stage managers may come and go, but the prompt book is forever. Some directors are known for keeping their prompt books in a safe when not in use. It is not considered being overly cautious.

In a high school or community theatre production, the director oftentimes acts as the stage manager until performance nights. For what better purpose can a first-class prompt book be prepared than to serve one's own interest? Or the director may find a capable theatre student to be the stage manager or assistant to the director for the pro-

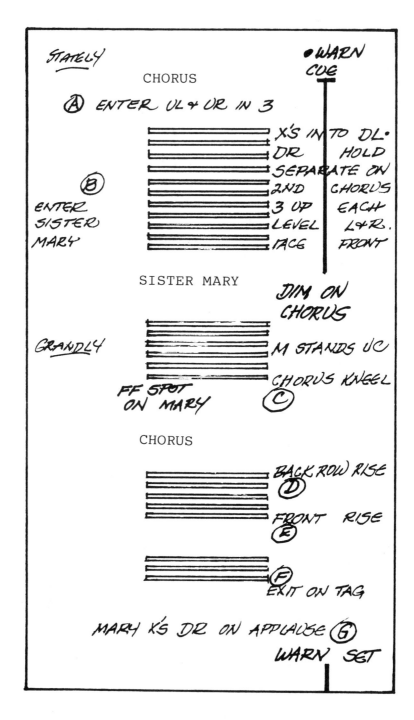

Fig. 8.17. Diagram of a musical number.

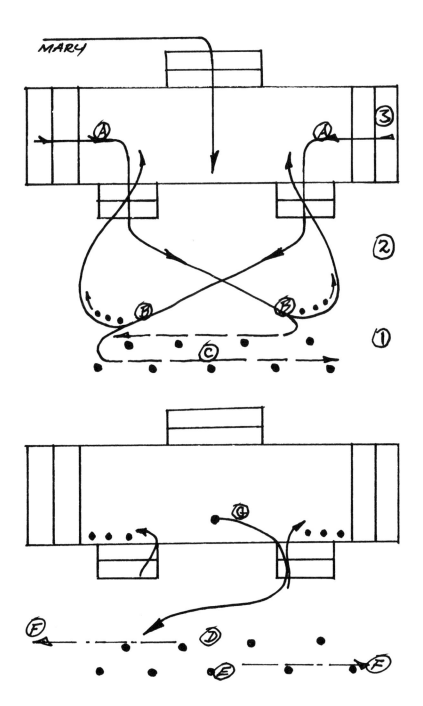

Fig. 8.18. Diagram of a musical number.

duction. As in professional theatre, this student may work with a prompt book side-by-side with the director throughout the rehearsal period. That student receives an excellent education in solid, classic theatre.

The prompt book may serve as the repository for anything and everything the director feels goes with the show, for example, the rehearsal schedule.

Generally, the director will paste a copy of the rehearsal schedule inside the front cover of the prompt book.

On a recent visit to the Metropolitan Opera House in New York City, where some of author Boland's former students are employed in stage managing, lighting, and carpentry, he was able to view the prompt books kept on file for the opera repertory. Inches thick, each book details every possible notation of what occurs in a given opera. Exacting descriptions for the scenic hanging plots as well as lighting instructions for each piece of equipment and its use are recorded.

There are also notations of previous errors or mishaps to be avoided in the future. All actions and stage business, carefully recorded with music directions, are documented for future remounting of an opera.

These extraordinary books, complete with detailed color photographs, are kept in fireproof vaults. Need anything else be said about the value and virtue of a well-done prompt book?

Chapter 9
The Stage Picture

The fundamental building blocks of a production are the choices a director makes for stage movements. Careful attention must be paid to this task that will later support the actor's playing, focus, and business.

While at first glance it may seem entirely too simplistic to reduce stage movement to five to ten possible dialogue motivations, or combinations thereof, the end product is practical and effective.

In this process, think of yourself as the eyes of the audience. What do you really want the audience to know or discover as the play progresses? The dialogue and music are not there merely to entertain or simply move things along; they carry meanings and ideas that capture our attention and imagination. Everything you set in motion, each action by the actors, must convey something vital to the play. Question yourself often, "I wonder what the audience will think of that?" If an action or arrangement doesn't serve the purpose of the material at hand, don't do it!

Visual Arrangements

Theatre, from the Greek *theatron,* is a "seeing place." It follows that what we do must be visual. We should be able to look at the stage picture and action without obstructions, either scenic or human. Ensemble groups mustn't obscure important action, and the incorrect placement of doors and sightlines must be avoided.

The meaning and the purpose of staging are brought to us by our sense of sight and directed to appropriate parts of the brain. Part of this is accomplished by visual design. You can improve your production by following some of the fundamental laws of design.

Five Concepts

One way to grasp some of these principles is to think of your flat stage floor as a two-dimensional surface. On such a plane, for example, the page of a magazine or a poster, or even a fine art painting, certain concepts apply:

- Absolute symmetry is static (fig. 9.1).

- Occult symmetry has more interest (fig. 9.2).

- Imbalance is more like nature (fig. 9.3).

- Curvilinear movement is more rhythmic (fig. 9.4).

- Texture adds interest (fig. 9.5).

A triangular arrangement (fig. 9.6) always creates a point of focus. Have you noticed that bridges and buildings are strongest when based on the triangle principle? A circle is graceful but vulnerable to pressure; a square may bend with weight; but a triangle is able to withstand pressure from all points.

We use the triangle effectively on stage (and in drawings and paintings) by

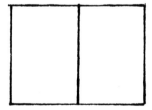

Fig. 9.1. Static/absolute symmetry.

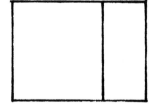

Fig. 9.2. Imbalance/occult symmetry.

Fig. 9.3. Natural imbalance.

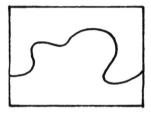

Fig. 9.4. Wave-like curvilinear.

considering how to arrange crowds or group actors in a conversation. Even after breaking a triangle for blocking conforming to our motivations, we can immediately restore it.

The virtue of the triangle concept in staging your actors is the creation of a pleasing "picture," regardless of other elements such as scenery. Your scenic artist has probably already used such balances in creating the stage design.

Weight and Balance

It is useful to think of your stage picture as an old-fashioned balance scale. A weight too heavy on one side unbalances the scale. We can, however, maintain balance if equal weights of unequal sizes are pitted against each other (fig. 9.7).

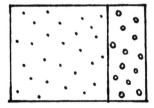

Fig. 9.5. Textural interest.

Fig. 9.6. Circle-square-triangle.

Fig. 9.7. Imbalance/balance.

The same thing is true for the placement and arrangement of actors. Begin in your mind's eye with actors placed in a perfect semi-circle (fig. 9.8), which, incidentally, used to be the standard method for staging chorus numbers in operettas and Gilbert and Sullivan productions. Imagining the semi-circle as ideal for seeing and hearing, you can begin to invent ways to deviate from this to achieve greater variety.

There are times when your staging will benefit from a formal design. Courtly scenes, formal dances, graduation assemblies, ceremonial events, or a mimicry (satire) of these same examples may all be handled in a traditional arrangement. An occasional formal scene, if motivated by the script, provides a moment of variety or seriousness (fig. 9.9).

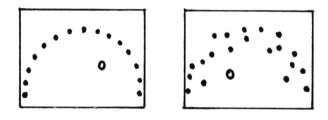

Fig. 9.8. Semicircle.

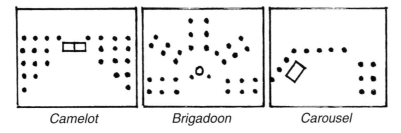

Fig. 9.9. Formal arrangements for *Camelot, Brigadoon,* and *Carousel.*

Variety

There is another area of design that is important for creating stage groupings. We have briefly suggested ways to utilize principles of balance and emphasis. Now consider an all-too-common fault with nonprofessional productions: lack of variety.

Unity and Variety

When the playwright's task is done properly, the situations are varied. The dialogue shows both character and emotional variation. The requirements of a given scene (beats) are never like a previous scene. We need variety.

The principle of theatrical variety must, of necessity, be part of a greater unity. The recognition of unity and variety as part of daily experience can be traced back to the ancient Greeks, who made this principle a part of their art and philosophy. The Greeks' search for an understanding of this phenomenon led to developments in classic drama and art. Consider a few examples of unity and variety before we apply the ideas to musical staging.

Unities	*Varieties*
Twenty-four hours in a day	Morning, afternoon, evening, night
The human species	Male, female; differing body types
A symphony	Sonata, scherzo, minuet, coda
A painting (one scene)	Relationship of theme, tone, style

In the visual and graphic arts, such a concept is essential, and theatre, after all, is a visual art.

Application

One positive result from your use of some of these ideas is style. If you ask yourself whether a grouping or staging is consistent, you stand a better chance of giving your production an overall quality or style of its own. A clear application of style resulting from chosen design elements can be easily seen in the musical *Brigadoon*.

Brigadoon is a town where everyone must share a common goal. The town comes "to life" once every hundred years. The action of the story emphasizes living. Lerner and Loewe clearly chose to create Scots-like musical numbers that are uniformly up-tempo, upbeat, or uplifting. They certainly reinforce the "live it up" theme. The action songs or numbers are similarly sung and danced animatedly, yet they also provide variety. A swirling, spontaneous, joyous scene in MacConnachy Square is punctuated with laughter and dancing. A preparation-for-marriage scene anticipates life and motherhood.

Later, these same villagers are dressed splendidly for a wedding dance, a physically demanding, formal, but active ceremony. At the same time, the scene is warm and touching. In sharp contrast, the audience sees a wild, energetic chase through the forest—and a tragic death. Then, we are treated to a wedding party where everyone has gotten a bit inebriated, and the same lively spirit serves up a comic, devil-may-care musical number. Again, all is done in the interest of life and continuity.

For a further, possibly richer extension of this principle we are transported out of Scotland to New York City, where all is cynical, pointless, and dull.

A startling lack of unity occurred in a college production of this same play. The director thought he could get laughs, and be different, by staging the haunting, tragic chase scene and subsequent death of Harry Beaton in Act II with strobe lights, which gave it an oldtime Keystone Cops effect. The audience did laugh, though nervously. This staging destroyed the entire meaning of a very beautiful play. When the death of Harry was announced in the necessary song setting, most of the audience roared. It was a wrong directorial decision.

Thinking your production through very thoroughly will provide imaginative revelations for staging possibilities. Your director's sixth sense becomes the force for making an integrated, unified production. We have all seen shows where individual scenes and single performances were brilliant but the entire production lacked focus.

Pondering which musical numbers ought to get the most staging helps avoid common mistakes. If you make the opening number in *Hello, Dolly* your major production number with show-stopping action, you may never be able to top it. Comments on different musical numbers appear later.

Good directing often comes from making good judgments, those "perfect" choices.

Chapter 10
Auditions and Casting

Casting is somewhat like trying to guess which key in a boxful will open a particular lock. It's a split second call made up from instinct, experience, and prejudice. Sometimes the lock opens and reveals an electric performance. Other times a lot of oil is needed to hide the squeaks. And sometimes you hope the audience will accept the mere fact that a lock and a key, although they may not work together, have some sort of relationship.

Auditions and casting for all shows must be intense and serious. Does this mean you can't enjoy the process? Far from it. One shouldn't trifle with the hopes of a budding actor, however.

An efficient, skillfully handled casting call may set the tone for the entire production. Be sure of yourself. Be certain of your material. Be confident about the requirements of the chosen production especially in terms of characters' goals and desires in life. If an actor displays a lack of concentration, objectivity, or a sense of sureness about himself, he cannot possibly play Harold Hill in *The Music Man*. Similarly, a Laurie in *Oklahoma!* who isn't a touch independent, stubborn, and perfectly capable of being on her own won't fit the role.

At an audition for a college production of *Irma La Douce* the director, with absolute confidence and much enthusiasm, described the plot of the show and the characters he wanted portrayed. The problem: he obviously had not read the script. What he described was the movie version of *Irma!* Thus, as students got up to read for parts, the plot that unfolded in the readings was not the Broadway show script. Needless to say, that director charged on. The result? A formless, UN-musical production.

The ability to sing a song on key may not be the only necessity of a role. Most characters in music theatre shows begin as antagonists to one another. Yet, their very opposition in type or desire is what may bring them together. Though Henry Higgins and Eliza Doolittle seem to be extreme opposites on a social scale, they nonetheless each want the same thing: a better quality of life from this world. One way this is expressed is in the way two songs—"Why Can't the English" and "Wouldn't It Be Loverly"—are juxtaposed. They are also counterpoints to one another. Try singing them together, and you'll understand.

In *The Music Man,* Harold Hill's braggadocio song "76 Trombones" contrasts with Marian Paroo's description of her ideal, responsible man in "My White Knight." Amazingly enough, though sung in different tempos and circumstances they are the same song melodically. You need to know such things in order to make knowledgeable, effective selections in casting.

Tryouts

If you have a musical director and a choreographer (and perhaps an orchestra conductor as well), be sure to include them in the casting process and discuss anticipated needs with them. Having these persons present is not the same thing as "committee casting" which we'll cover later.

Independent casting, where the choreographer may hold separate auditions, is just not a good idea. The singing or dancing ensemble should know who is in charge of the overall artistic production. If they don't, there may be a lack of cooperation with the staging director and a lack of respect. So, take a week of afternoons, or several nights, if need be, and include all of your working staff members in the casting process. Everyone will feel more positive about the production.

Ideally, actors should be able to read the script ahead of auditions. It will give them a good sense of the roles they are suited for. More than likely, however, you will have only one production script, and auditioners will not have read the play or understood it ahead of tryouts. It is particularly democratic to give everyone a try at all the parts. It encourages and provides experience. But, artistically and practically, it is distracting and unproductive. Be aware that problems may arise at your auditions because of the disparity between the age of the character and the actor's age. Head off disappointment and opposition by clearly stating in your presentation what you are looking for in your casting. It will avoid offending people and hurting feelings. In Gilbert and Sullivan's *The Mikado,* the schoolgirls are between eighteen and twenty years of age. Older female singers don't fit—unless you really intend to spoof the spoof.

Begin with a concise, orderly description of your show. Give a clear recitation of the plot, providing as much of the spirit and flavor of the time, place, and action as you can. Seventeenth-century Scotland in *Brigadoon* or Biblical times in *Joseph and the Amazing Technicolor Dreamcoat* convey as much of the atmosphere and feeling you are after as the plots do.

Hand out as many choral parts as you have. Make a stab at singing a typical, colorful, catchy production number. Often it's a good way to enhance the telling of the plot and partially overcomes feelings of fear or being in the dark about the story!

Another effective way to break the ice is to select the most typical musical number—often a male or female separate song—and have everyone, still seated, sing it together. Make this process both informative and instructive. Point out after the first singing where there might be more emphasis, enthusiasm, clear enunciation, or careful attention to rhythm, and so on. Immediately, this opens the door to direction, and because they are in a group, actors tend not to take it as criticism. People pay attention more immediately, and YOU are already taking shape as a director!

Now get all or half, depending on numbers, of the female singers up together on the stage or around the piano. Sing the song again.

Continue this process, using fewer singers each time until you are down to three or four. Listen to them carefully, because now you are seeking possible lead roles. Put another group of four together and then another; this familiarizes everyone with the song and overcomes stage fright or fear of the director.

This technique also gives you (and a music director) a good grasp of the vocal ranges available and who has the strongest voices. You will find quite frequently that this procedure actually encourages people to get up and sing solo in front of the other auditioners. The same process also works effectively for dancers.

If you have the luxury of time on your side, schedule solo or principal auditions for another time. This way the possible cast have had one night of experience and are much more confident when reading and singing at a second audition.

Protect feelings where you can. Hurt feelings and jealousies are bound to occur simply because most people who audition care as much for the production as you do, or they wouldn't be there. Do be understanding. It may pay dividends later. This especially refers to assigning or denying roles in front of others.

> Our adage: Hold the auditions in public; make the assignments in private.

Here's an example of a failed auditioner's reaction. An actor with a thick southern accent trashed the director's office when she tried out for, and didn't get, the role of Miss Adelaide in *Guys and Dolls*. As the two of them, together, cleaned up the disarray the next day, they talked. Another year, after some speech training, the actor played the role of Eliza Doolittle and went on to success in summer theatre and teaching. She and the director are still friends.

Take the time then to let the hopeful tryouts down easily, either with another role or some encouraging words.

At the outset of auditions, remind those assembled that not everyone can have a major part; not everyone may be cast this time. The talented freshman or sophomore can be encouraged to be an understudy in preparation for future productions.

If one is working with a community theatre, college, or high school group, make it a practice to suggest proper dress for auditioning. A black silk, split skirt dress may be fine for *Sweet Charity,* but it is out of place for *Hello, Dolly.*

Given the dress fads and codes of the nineties, people are apt to show up in clothes that deny you the ability to see how they walk, sit, move, and, in general, what they really look like. Students in high school may perhaps be cautioned ahead of time to dress for auditions. Usually, however, they will show up in the clothes they've worn to school. At one time wooden clogs were the vogue. Just try to concentrate, or listen to, someone reading lines or singing a romantically gentle song accompanied by a clomping tattoo on a wooden floor.

If the roles are "girlish," advise actors to dress for it. If the roles are for the men in *West Side Story,* you need to see the whole body of the actor. To be sure, knowledge of "dressing for the part" will help budding actors should they ever audition professionally.

If there is anything more nerve-wracking than casting the musical show, it is hard to say what it might be. Casting is a contradiction in itself. It is a quite subjective task but must be approached with absolute objectivity. Casting usually takes place early in the year, when you know the least about your actors. In community theatre, friendships may be lost or won. In school productions, favorite scholars may be expecting rewards for academic excellence by getting a lead role. The size of your cast is also an element fraught with dangerous possibilities.

Double-casting

Many schools may have an unwritten policy that everyone who tries out must be included in the final ensemble. If your production is a Gilbert and Sullivan piece, you might—and we stress *might*—be able to accommodate a cast of forty or fifty. It will drastically increase your costume budget, however. Likewise, *Bye Bye Birdie* may benefit from a large cast because of the subject and its treatment.

Author Boland has produced and directed both *Oklahoma!* and *The Music Man,* each with a cast of one hundred. The first was done in a ballpark and the second on a basketball court, both with successful results. *The Farmer and the Cowman* and *Iowa Stubborn* had a wonderful true-to-life impact. *The Fantasticks,* or *Man of La Mancha,* certainly can't be overcrowded and still do justice to the artistry of the scripts.

Double-casting—the use of more ensemble than is really called for with one group performing on alternate performance nights or matinees—is a way some schools solve this problem. The drawbacks are obvious. It entails more rehearsal time and careful deliberation or selection of abilities among students.

The more serious dilemma is one of growth and development. All actors, even the pros, need at least three consecutive performances before an audience to gain a real sense of pace and intensity and an awareness of how an audience will react. In fact, three performances are hardly enough to gain the rhythm and grace of making a production work with complete skill. Note the Broadway practice of offering two to four weeks of previews (performances with an audience) before an official, critics' opening.

While double-casting is sometimes done to give eager students a theatre opportunity, it may not always have the best result. One can, of course, have crowd scenes in musicals or use only part of the ensemble in some numbers and part in others. These are perfectly acceptable solutions. *Oliver* lends itself to shorter actors (children) and a variety of society types. *My Fair Lady* has both cockneys and "swells."

Readings

"Readings," or simply listening to people read the dialogue, are usually conducted separately from—and after—the music auditions. This practice lets you know immediately whether or not a potential actor is able to handle the vocal requirements. There seems little sense in having lengthy and tiring readings from individuals unsuited to certain roles.

Reading the dialogue aloud for the first time from a script, also known as a "cold" reading, is daunting even for professionals. Start slowly and ask your actors to read for clarity of ideas. Make these suggestions:

- Show me that you can read and pronounce words.

- Give me your best diction.

- Look ahead and emphasize the intention of your line.

- Read with some enthusiasm.

- Make words sound like what they mean. Give them the wonderful example of the Wicked Witch in *The Wizard of Oz* who proclaims, "I'm melt-i—n—g!"

Readings may be conducted in a number of ways. Among them are

- Direct readings. Actors read from the actual script of the chosen production.

- Indirect readings. The actors use alternative (but similar) material. This is supposed to prevent typecasting or favoritism.

  A word on typecasting, a theatre byword. It refers to choosing an actor who has the right physique, look, or age and generally naturally behaves like the character in the play. Jimmy, the class clown, gets the lead in *A Funny Thing Happened on the Way to the Forum*. Sometimes it works, as it did when Anne Bancroft auditioned for Gitel in Bill Gibson's *Two for the Seesaw*. She walked in as Gitel personified, complete with New York accent and mannerisms, and got the part. Often, it doesn't.

- Improvisation. Actors are given situations similar in nature or circumstances to a script and are asked to invent their dialogue, illustrating how they would feel in a particular situation.

Direct readings take top billing. They are more efficient and quicker methods of casting.

Professionally, things are quite different. In professional theatre, star roles are generally cast by directors, producers, and playwrights through contact with actors' agents. Dance roles are often cast by virtue of a choreographer's past experience with certain performers. For professionals, sad to say, it is a case of whom you know. Ensemble parts, or the general singing and dancing choruses, are open auditions unflatteringly known as "cattle calls." Aspiring young singers/actors are given a brief audition, sometimes no more than eight measures of a song to demonstrate their talent to the several directors, stage manager, producer, and whomever. Dancers are auditioned in groups. The choreographer, or dance captain, may demonstrate a combination of steps, and ask the auditioners to repeat them.

When a certain vocal sound is heard, or a dancer has able qualities, those doing the casting make note (often by number), and those noticed are asked to return for callbacks at a later time. However, in professional theatre the diplomatic way of indicating a lack of interest is usually to say, "Don't call us, we'll call you."

Some school and college directors offer this kind of casting experience to students by having an open audition prior to the specific ones. Students may be given the chance to perform whatever they themselves choose and thus acquaint the director with their ability. If you do this, be sure to provide a very capable accompanist who can read any music at a glance and improvise tempos on demand.

No matter what methods you may use for casting, at some point, even before the casting procedure, have everyone fill out an audition form that reminds them to list all the possible conflicts, from sports to medical appointments to piano lessons. Stories abound of the leading man or woman announcing three, four, or five weeks into rehearsal, "Oh, next week I won't be here, it's vacation time on the Cape!" Directors never think of suicide at that point—only murder!

Some community theatre groups do casting by a committee plus the director. Usually this is done because the director is a non-member or hired professional. A three- or five-person group attends auditions and votes by ballot for the role players. Sometimes this works well; other times it doesn't.

May all your casting choices open the door for electric performances.

Chapter 11
Beginning Rehearsals

The first rehearsal should begin right after you have seriously started the prompt book and have successfully, if nervously, cast your production.

First, the rehearsal schedule. It runs through almost three months. It starts with auditions and ends with the final performance. Also included are dates to order backdrops and costumes; start running ads; issue press releases; start and complete set construction; and run cue-to-cue, technical, and dress rehearsals.

Without being rigid or intractable, it is a good idea to stick to your schedule once you see that it is working. Once you begin to fall behind anxiety sets in, and suddenly each person involved tries to play catch-up. When the song isn't ready, the choreographer may be held up, and when a scene isn't well planned out, the musical direction may suffer. When you have reached the point of polishing the performance, the whole process of rehearsing may have to slow down a bit. Plan for those lost days well ahead of time.

Whether because of community theatre costs or school scheduling, it is probably not possible to unite the entire cast and the orchestra musicians until the very last days, often only at the dress rehearsal. Your directing goals ought to have been thoroughly achieved by this time. We will discuss rehearsals, along with "peaking" and "slumping," a bit later.

Before getting into the specifics of your first meeting, some suggestions. Enter into this period with confidence and enthusiasm, but temper everything with a firm sense of discipline and respect for the "art" of theatre. These two apparent abstracts are, in fact, related and tangible things.

Russian composer Igor Stravinsky said, "The more art is limited, the more it is controlled, the freer it is."

In an era when we have come to understand that every expression of human emotion and experience is valid and defensible, this statement seems contradictory, oxymoronic, even ambivalent.

Our interpretation is that the more completely you can master your craft, the more creative you can be in practicing it. Imagination is a wonderful thing, but without the knowledge of how to do something, or to make dreams facts, imagination may only be dreaming. Could Beethoven have written symphonies if he didn't know the rules of musical tonality, meter, and instrumentation?

As a director, getting your cast to pay attention, be prompt, and stick to the task at hand is a first step toward creativity.

> Here's a theatre aphorism that may humorously set the tone you want: "If you ain't early, you're late!"

Some directors will not reprimand a cast or crew for lateness, missing rehearsals, missing cues, or forgetting props. The reason? They want everyone to have "a good time" and to make theatre "fun." The fun in any artistic endeavor comes from accomplishment and pride. Being responsible for yourself and your work is an important part of the craft. You can be firm without being mean. You can be commanding without being demanding. To start, start off right! If you call a rehearsal for a specific hour, start exactly on time. Latecomers very soon catch on. In college, some professor-directors cast on Thursday night, hold a reading on Friday, and expect the actors to learn their parts by Monday night.

Above all, be efficient. If scripts need numbering for assignment and return after the production, do it ahead of time.

Have a schedule prepared for distribution even if it only covers one or two weeks' time. Prepare rehearsal schedules even before auditions are called. Distribute them to everyone who tries out so they will know what is expected of them—a commitment of time to an efficient, serious director.

First Rehearsal

Your initial rehearsal should begin with introductions. Cast and crew should know each other and the roles or tasks they are responsible for. First, they should know who you are and get a glimpse of how easy (or not) it will be to work with you. Take this opportunity for a little public relations work, give a pep talk for the production, and describe the wonderful opportunity they have all been given. Give your cast a lesson in professionalism regarding the extension of authority by introducing your staff next; for example, by presenting your stage manager as your "second right hand." Does everyone know the musical director? The accompanist? The choreographer?

Assume nothing. Tell cast and crew what you expect and that if they have a problem it should be discussed with you. Perhaps you need to remind them about choosing comfortable rehearsal clothes to dance in or remembering that the closeness of group activity demands a little hygiene.

Now, how do you get the cast really interested and "into" the show?

The Sing-along

This first rehearsal should be a "sing-along."

If you do not have scripts for each person in the cast, try to seat people so that they can follow dialogue and lyrics together. An overhead projector may be useful.

Have the whole cast, singers and dancers, sing all the musical numbers, even though some of the songs may be love songs for two lead characters. This activity makes them familiar with the musical style of the production, and, more importantly, they will learn something. The lyrics explain the plot and the action taking place. Briefly explain what the stage setting may look like as you encounter each scene.

Some directors maintain that the sing-along method may mislead people into getting the melody line into their heads and deter the learning of parts in chorus numbers. We do not consider this a problem, especially with a musical director or accompanist who makes the point that at the third rehearsal the cast will be separated into parts.

The purpose of a sit-down reading—professionally termed as well as used—such as this is to explain any dialogue, word, or place that might be unfamiliar. Is there a term in French or Russian, a city in Hungary or Australia that colors an actor's line? Ask them if they can give it meaning. If not, explain it. At the same time, be judicious with your explanations. You can get too lengthy and take too much precious time at first rehearsals. Everyone must know as much as possible about the play you are undertaking. A first reading with a sing-along should make the story understandable to the cast so that they can later tell it to the audience.

A second rehearsal, done exactly the same way with everyone joining in the musical pieces, should place some emphasis on the play's characters. Explain how they are motivated in a given scene.

Ask Questions Now

Questions or problems about interpreting the story and the mood atmosphere of each scene can be addressed so that a song might be sung more quietly or boisterously as suitable.

All-inclusive sing-along rehearsals are not usual in the professional theatre, lengthy "reading" sessions with much question-and-answering being the norm. Amateurs would do well to try to grasp the idea that the sing-along is their time to discuss—at length if need be—questions of interpretation and characterization, even on very subtle levels. Subsequent blocking and line learning rehearsals can then be devoted to their purposes to a much greater advantage.

Bedlam may result when a director attempts to block a scene, impart meaningful psychological suggestions of character, direct actors in learning lyrics, and create stage business. Too often, everyone involved, especially the director, feels that they must hasten the business of getting "on with the show." In your anxiety to forge ahead, haste may make waste! After completing the groundwork described above, you can move on to blocking, our first look at the show as the audience will eventually view it.

Chapter 12
Learning Blocking

How does a director convey blocking to the actors? Various methods exist. If you come up with a technique for giving blocking to actors that works for you and makes you comfortable, use it! Remember that blocking can always be changed.

Here are some methods:

- Summer stock blocking. Designed for working efficiently and rapidly.

- Improvisational or repertory blocking. Developed for actors who work together in successive productions, usually in continuous performance situations.

- Traditional blocking. Used by directors who prefer to create a unique style with a certain unity and control. Also very efficient.

Summer Stock Blocking

Using the "summer stock" technique, sit your actors down and dictate each bit of blocking either as you have recorded it in your prompt book or as it appears in the script. Each actor records the blocking given, using the theatre shorthand of UC, DR, and so on. An "X" indicates a cross from one area of the stage to another. The direction X to UL and Exit C door should make perfect sense. An "X" in a box means "sit here."

The process is very efficient if you dictate at a moderate pace and then get up and rehearse each scene as instructed.

The obvious objection experienced directors have to this technique is that it deprives both the director and actor of a really personal feeling about blocking and would seem to reduce the art to a mechanical function.

Repertory Blocking

Improvisational, or repertory, technique is most effective with very experienced actors. This kind of "exercise" rehearsal is very helpful in making the leap from readings to actual staging, no matter what technique you may finally adopt. The director says, "Let's just do the dialogue and scene as written, and, observing the set levels, stairs, or furniture, you people move around as freely as you like or do whatever feels right for your character."

Be sure that the actors realize that whatever happens may not be the final blocking. The director might add, "I think we will do the whole script this way, simply as an exercise to help us become very familiar with the script and its needs."

Because this blocking is actor-spontaneous, take a moment to check your prompt book.

Let's assume you have carefully constructed your prompt book and that you have followed the suggestions in the previous chapter. Thus, your blocking is notated and coordinated with the dialogue in the script with the beats duly marked with appropriate actions such as exits and entrances.

It is fascinating to see that a great many of your well-thought-out analyses for blocking are what the actor is apt to do on his own. It illustrates the fact that human beings do have almost physically instinctive ways of reacting to events they encounter. The good director is always searching out these responses. If you see an action you feel really helps the impact or dramatic intent of a scene, make a note, and keep it in your script.

Traditional Blocking

Using either of the previous approaches should only take up one or two rehearsals. Now you have to get down to putting everything in perspective and set the chosen blocking in place just as it will be during the performance. Actors need to be sure of exactly where another actor will be if they are to develop proper objectives and emotional feeling. Honest, believable reaction is impossible in a scene or song if a partner isn't fully involved.

Chapter 13
Conducting Rehearsals

Your actors are on their feet, ready to act. What's the next step? Give them the blocking from your prompt book.

Give the Blocking

First, tell them that "tonight we will just be concerned with getting the blocking for our dialogue. Songs and chorus scenes will come later. As we start the dialogue, I will stop you often just before an action is to take place. This way you can (lightly) write your blocking directly in your script where it happens." You might add, "This may be a very slow process, and we will only cover as many scenes as are possible tonight, but if we get it right this time, we can learn our lines sooner and start developing the show's qualities."

Step-by-Step

When you're beginning blocking rehearsals, try to remember Plato's allegory of the cave and his description of how we learn best in a step-by-step process.

Here's a sample of this rehearsal taking place between the director and actors Harold and Mary:

Director

OK, Harold, you are standing DL looking out over the audience. Go.

Harold

"Gosh, Mary, you oughta see this view!"

Director (interrupting)

Be sure you are looking at the view yourself and convince us you can really see it. Mary, before you reply, X to DR away from Harold.

Mary

"Oh! I've seen plenty of mountain views before."

Director

X to Mary on this, Harold, be exasperated.

Harold

"Doesn't anything impress you?"

Director

Mary, sit on your next line.

Mary

"Not much. I'm just bored."

It probably strikes you that this is going to take a long time. What is going to happen, however, is that very soon your actors will begin to "feel" the process at work, and they will learn to respond quickly. In almost no time at all, you are offering your directions briefly and efficiently. For example:

- "Cross L on this."

- "Take her arm, and X DL when you say this."

- "Sit on that."

- "Stand to start the song."

After you have worked with your actors for a period of time, you often merely need to nod your head or point in a specific direction, "up the stairs," or to a scenic feature, such as a rock or tree, and they will respond and record it quickly. If they get ahead of you, and the visual arrangement doesn't appear to be working or there is confusion because an actor ends up standing in front of someone else, just stop everything and go back to where the confusion occurred.

Another trick that actually works as a technique for giving everyone—including yourself—a breathing space is to pause whenever a song is going to be introduced and remind, "OK, when we stage this number at the next rehearsal, Harold will do the introduction from the steps, and Mary will finish the number downstage right where Harold will join her, so we can take it from there, and go on." A short break after two or three scenes, along with words of praise for their effort and cooperation, will also do wondrous things for a cast.

Rehearsing Song Sequences

Skipping over the song sequences when you are busy blocking the principals gives the music director an opportunity to begin work on the ensemble numbers. This also keeps the whole cast occupied during what has to be a slow process. No matter the age of the cast, unless they are professionals being paid for this activity, people will get restless wondering when their turn will come.

Likewise, when you are blocking your leads, the choreographer may be mounting the dance steps and instructing dancers. If the dancers and the singers are the same persons, as in *Annie* where the orphans all sing and dance, you may have to alternate sequences.

After the initial blocking rehearsals are completed you may decide that it will feel better to complete all of Act I before attacking Act II. If so, begin blocking the musical numbers at the next rehearsal or two.

Still, it's a beneficial thing to "run" briefly the dialogue blocked in the previous rehearsals, keeping in mind that you want to concentrate on the musical staging at this point.

Attention to Detail

As you develop your general staging of everything at this step in rehearsals, watch for little bits of business that will enhance a given scene or performance. If you make note of a "turn of the head," a spontaneous shift of "focus," or the need to suggest an actor can get a better response by a sudden "surprise" line delivery, you can add these elements in at later rehearsals.

Don't just pay attention to what you want them to do; watch carefully for things they will do on the spot that might give you ideas to be developed further on. Take full advantage of those idiosyncratic characteristics and personality traits that attract us to one another in real life. Great "stars" are usually the people with warm, charming, and gregarious personalities. When that special quality reaches over the footlights we—the audience—are captivated and responsive.

Chapter 14
Rehearsal Techniques

By the time you are into musical staging, you are also well along in your rehearsal schedule. It is already time to think constantly of the finished product.

Everything the actors and ensemble do conveys a message or some kind of information to the audience. One only need watch a good TV commercial to know that we constantly respond subliminally to movement, gesture, tone of voice, and action.

Is the ensemble really listening to the spoken dialogue? Are they reacting with appropriate cognition, awe, surprise, or whatever?

Stay Fresh

A very real danger in amateur productions is the comfortable feeling that the actors know their lines and scenes extremely well. Often, they know them so well that the dramatic quality of "this is happening for the first time" is missing.

> Whether an actor is the lead role or in the third line of the chorus, the original spontaneity must be recreated in every rehearsal and every performance.

Most musicals have such a compact, integrated relationship between libretto and score that we seldom feel a sense of "dragging," or sluggishness. The playwrights and composers are usually skillful enough to introduce up-tempo numbers at strategic moments to give a show the boost it needs.

There are exceptions to the rule. *Camelot,* even for professionals, is a l-o-n-g show.

So is *Hello, Dolly*. If the actors do not keep up a brisk, bright pace of dialogue, it makes for a long evening, and audiences find an excuse—the baby sitter, the weather—to leave early.

All the more reason for the director to remind actors in rehearsal to "pick up your cues." This simply means that two or more people engaged in dialogue will respond quickly (or not, if the scene dictates) to the lines spoken to them. Any conversation, in real or stage life, is more exciting if it isn't labored or cluttered with awkward pauses.

The Musical Moment

It bears repeating here that the unusual relationship between dialogue, music, and/or dance is a unique feature of the musical show. Think about how this balance works. Remind yourself of earlier comments on why we sing in a musical. We sing because our emotions or circumstances have reached such a peak that we must act them out physically (through dance) or proclaim them beyond mere speech (through song).

Carefully study the lines of dialogue leading into, and out of, a musical number. Compelling a person to sing or dance suggests that speeches must gather more intensity as the musical moment arrives. Sometimes the lines must be faster to convey excitement or delivered with more emphasis to create the tension, especially if there is music played "under" the specific dialogue. It follows that a more serious contemplative scene may gain its intensity from a possible slowing of dialogue prior to a more serious, insightful musical moment. This moment, however, is rare.

Focus

A difficult task for the director is remembering to create a focus, a place where you expect and plan for the audience to look. This may be difficult only because the director is constantly "on top of" the actors in the rehearsal process. We don't often step back until the final stages of polishing and combining the orchestra with actors.

You always know where to place your attention because you know the script, the score, and who's doing what. The show is new to an audience, however, so they must be shown where to shift their attention. You need to do this to provide the necessary expository steps toward making the play's theme and character clear and, sometimes, just to make the story/plot understandable. The audience will look wherever their attention is focused.

Every reliable text on play directing has addressed the question of focus. Research reviews time-honored practices that may be reduced to ten situations that direct focus.

We tend to focus, or direct our attention to an actor, if

- The actor is the one speaking

- The actor is the one alone or isolated from a group

- The actor is the one on a different level

- The actor is pointed out by the others facing the actor

- The actor is being rejected by others moving away

- The actor is the one kneeling, or fallen, or differentiated in any way

- The actor is the one who is unusual by way of costume, lighting, or a "character" walk or action

- The actor is placed in a strong downstage, or upstage, position

- The actor is the one we wait to hear from expectantly, perhaps because of the character's motivation

- The actor is the one whose reactions or "stage business" the director makes us want to see

In a Broadway production, we tend, of course, to look at someone who is a major "star," or the title character, such as Billy Bigelow in *Carousel* or J. Pierpont Finch in *How to Succeed in Business without Really Trying*. Most of the time stars have such attractive appearances or magnetic personalities that we cannot, as they say, "take our eyes off them." It's charisma, star quality, that works.

A last comment, but a most important one. Focus must be intrinsic to the meaning of the dialogue. It should make an emphatic statement about the plot.

The Vision of the Show

With bright, young, energetic students or enthusiastic, devoted amateurs, it is almost easy to charm an audience into accepting a nicely done musical production. The well-tried and proven property is itself a major factor in your favor. We would like to believe, however, that there will be a greater goal in mind. Namely, to construct a piece of theatre that will awaken the talents of those involved and illuminate the mind of the audience. Peter Brook, in an interview in *American Theatre Magazine* (April 1995), while not referring specifically to musicals, says this: "If the theatre . . . liberates the audience, even for a few hours . . . and [makes them] confront not only the contradictions of life, but also the continuum of horrors . . . then it helps people live their lives in a better way."

Your vision of the play, and the attempt to make that vision a reality, will accomplish this. Your means, or method, is in the hands of the actors. How will you help them do this? As inferred above, the abilities and attractiveness of your cast is almost guaranteed to please an audience. Therein lies danger. We will like them all so much, being familiar with them as kids or people we know, we can accept nearly anything. It is necessary for the director to have already established an agenda for seeing that actors will not just recite clever lines they have learned by rote.

There is a long period of time between the blocking and the dress rehearsals. What are the activities during this period? Learning lines, learning music, staging numbers, integrating those production numbers, and making room for dancers. But there is another level to the director's job. That is, to make clear, through the actors/dancers/singers, the objective of the show.

Your objectives as director are relatively simple:

- Stage the production

- Rehearse the actors

- Assimilate, combine, and organize the scenes

- Orchestrate the elements of music and dance

- Bring everything to a point of operation

- "Make it happen"

As you are manipulating and moving through these steps, you have a responsibility to the actors. You must cajole, coerce, or remind them to

- Establish their own objectives

- Respect and remember the beats of a scene

- Stay in character at all times

- Pick up cues (from the previous speech)

- Respond in character with intentions

- Maintain a pace, a rhythm appropriate to *this* show

- Remember to "lead" into songs with meaning

- Make the scenes fresh, new, and spontaneous every time

- Learn the lines and lyrics

None of this is easy. If it were, no one would write books about theatre direction.

Neglect of these elements makes a show amateurish. Let's examine some ways to bring them into your production. First, whether directing a straight play or a musical, re-read the script by yourself once a week. Even though one sees it acted out at each rehearsal, a careful reinspection is refreshing. After suitable singing or acting warm-ups to shake off the more mundane distractions of daily life and energize the cast, a quiet moment of instruction is beneficial.

It is vital that you work with your script and constantly set objectives to be achieved at each rehearsal.

Each time, tell everyone just what you need to accomplish. For instance, you might say, "I realize that we are still trying to remember blocking and feeling our way around. We haven't even staged our songs and musical numbers, but it is essential that we begin to think about how we will play a scene. The beats we have marked off should help each of you know why your scene is in the script. At this rehearsal you should try to stay in character at all times. Listen to the person playing opposite you as if you had never heard them say the line before. Try to react with genuine interest and freshness."

You might try a different tactic. "Well, you have accomplished a great deal in three weeks. Most of us are sure of our blocking and are off book, which is terrific. Tonight let's concentrate on picking up cues. No pauses in between speeches, because pauses tend to drag the pace. Besides, bright, witty, alert characters such as those you are playing needn't think arduously or methodically about what to say next. Keep the spirit of repartee and conversation building to your musical number."

You may wish to take this approach. "Listening to your dialogue, I'm not always sure of your intentions. Sometimes questions don't sound as if you are asking for information. Don't let your voice take a sing-song pattern. Nobody (except maybe TV sitcom actors) repeats everything the same." To let student actors see how their speech flow is uniquely their own, point out speech patterns. Reading poetry aloud is a good way to detect the rise and fall of inflections.

The stage director must show how characters' emotions color the dialogue in order to keep it from being boring or uninformative. Don't let all the ends of lines end the same. Being aware of beats and putting emphasis on the "objective" of a piece of dialogue overcomes this.

A reminder of what the theatrical meaning of objective is would be helpful. According to Webster, an objective is something that one's efforts and actions are intended to attain or accomplish. Its purpose, goal.

For the actor the objective is the motivation that makes a character say whatever he says. In acting classes, we learn that in real life every movement, reaction, choice of words, or nuance of language or facial expression establishes objectives. When you automatically reach for the door handle or flatten out your hand in a raised position, it is to open a door. When you open your eyes widely and raise your voice, it is to express your anger or your surprise. Scratching your skin after a mosquito bite seems reflexive, but in reality it is a kind of learned objective to relieve an itch. Your actors need to find, with your help, the objectives that make their characters real.

No two scenes can be the same. Director Constantin Stanislavsky accompanied a friend to the theatre where a famous actress was appearing. She was to play a commanding maternal role. Afterwards, the director asked his friend what he thought of her performance. "Ah!" said the friend, "I thought she was *my* mother." Stanislavky's reply was, "Then she failed because, of course, she was *not* your mother."

Seeing It Happen

Critics, reviewers, naysayers notwithstanding, the fact that a school, community, or college performance gets on the boards at all is nearly miraculous. Each of us has been moved or thrilled enough by an amateur production enough to proclaim it "almost professional!"

Consider, however, that a trained, experienced professional performer may rehearse for five or six hours at a time, with a concentration not always possible with school students or community actors. After all, families, exams, doctor appointments, sports, and bus schedules are very real. The professional rehearsal period is usually four weeks (or more) for a total of eighty to 160 hours. The average amateur production is fortunate if it can rehearse three hours an evening or after school for maybe eight to twelve weeks. Add all this up, and we find that the amateur expends seventy to ninety hours rehearsing—much of which must be spent teaching actors to act, dancers to dance, singers to sing. The "almost" or "as good as" performance is consequently an amazing occurrence.

The Difference

Perhaps the major difference between the professional and the amateur actor is that a professional actor, guided by a professional director, knows exactly when a line or a piece of business is "right" and does not change it arbitrarily. How else can it be that classic, award-winning productions can go on for years and years and not lose their freshness? One often hears, "Oh! I'll do better with an audience out there." Precision and mastery of acting and singing are what make an accomplished performance, not the presence of an audience. The admonition, then, to the beginning actor is to establish objectives. Try to understand the character's hidden intention. Attempt to interpret the driving motivation. Once that essential action or vocalization has been captured, make it yours, and do not lose it.

The late Mary Martin once said that she usually composed the next day's grocery list in her head while singing "Climb Every Mountain" onstage. This, despite the fact that she was required to cry real tears and express deep emotion at the same time. Because her actor's training and her body responses were so involved in her presentation of the song, there was never a second's variance in her singing or a false motion of her body. How does an actor teach himself to accomplish such accuracy of thought and response? Go to a private, quiet place and rehearse—for hours, if need be. In the professional theatre they call it "woodshedding." In another era "going to the woodshed" related strictly to discipline, something the professional learns early on. It's great advice for the young actor: go woodshedding!

Another thought for the young actor/performer comes from Francis Bacon (1561–1626), the English philosopher and essayist, who said, "The job of the artist is always to deepen the mystery." This sounds obscure, but it can be interpreted to mean that the painter, poet, or actor who intrigues our minds and captivates and stimulates our imagination forces us, the audience, to go further with our discovery of the meanings of human life.

The job of the director is to help "deepen the mystery."

Chapter 15
The Musical Number

Technology has transformed the musical show. You might have seen the revolution taking place if you visited Broadway during the 1990s. The concept of what a musical "might" be like was forever changed by technology. Even the revivals of old standards such as *Damn Yankees, How to Succeed in Business without Really Trying, Carousel, Grease, Hello, Dolly,* and *Showboat* have been given new productions and fresh lives by directors' visions of them.

As it should be, new themes and ideas explore aspects of human behavior hitherto left to what we call legitimate theatre, or non-musical serious plays. *Kiss of the Spider Woman, Sunset Boulevard, Les Misérables,* and *Cats* are complex psychological expressions of our deepest needs. Perhaps we shall revise our historical definitions of the American musical and finally accept the true designation of "musical play" rather than the slightly derisive "musical comedy."

The Purpose of a Song

One hopes, as a director, that these changes will put to rest the practice of labeling the placement of musical incidents in a play as merely functional. While reading various texts on the musical show we have encountered these terms: opening number, production number, showstopper, star-turn. We have even seen a number designated a ballad, comedy, charm, or dramatic song. The clear implication is that these moments with music occur according to some wise FORMULA, which once known or discovered, makes it possible to write a musical show. As anyone who has tried to write a musical show knows, there is no formula. If there were, why would it be necessary for new productions "in trouble" out of town—or "Nix Fix In Sticks" as *Variety* might say—to call in highly paid experts, or play doctors, to do rewrites?

Broadly applied, labels may view the song only as a device, something inserted for purposes of entertainment only. If this were true, musicals would only be plays with some appealing songs added on.

Some of the musicals in our vast collection of shows have been successful because they do cleverly follow an established, proven technique. But they also happen to have been written by enormously talented authors such as Cole Porter, George Gershwin, and Lorenz Hart, to name a few. Even as "formula" shows, these works are wonderful gems of theatre.

It has always been popular with critics and biographers of Gilbert and Sullivan to refer to certain musical pieces as "patter songs." This is perhaps forgiveable because of the intense condensation of lyric and melody that Gilbert and Sullivan created. But even these patter songs are cleverly disposed revelations of characters' personalities and psyches. "When you're lying awake, with a dismal headache" is marvelous Freudian psychology with Jungian overtones, done by Gilbert and Sullivan. In fact, most of their musicals are profound expressions of nineteenth-century philosophies getting the ridicule they deserved (Darwin included), which is another matter entirely.

Another way of understanding the purpose of a song in the musical was suggested by Gower Champion, the brilliant director of *Bye Bye Birdie, Carnival, Hello, Dolly* and *42nd Street*. Champion referred to most musical solo numbers as "I want" songs. He defines these songs as describing what a character needs to live, indeed to be. He clearly felt, and demonstrated in his staging, that the song is the driving force of both plot and characters. Keeping this in mind prompts a stage director both to reflect and illustrate such motivation in the physical and emotional intensity he develops with the character and performer.

Technology and Innovation

Irrevocably tied to these ideas is the new "look" on Broadway, mentioned earlier. In modern musicals the staging of musical numbers is not only vocal but choreographic, and, in many, many cases, technological as well. Scenic elements rise and fall, elevators lift entire settings overhead, and, as in *Starlight Express,* actors roller skate effortlessly in and out of the audience. What ever happened to the good old days when only Peter Pan could fly? The musical star must today be part athlete, dancer, actor, and singer.

Much of this spectacular staging is only possible because we have sophisticated means of amplification. The era of song belters, such as Ethel Merman, is probably gone. "Belting" is nowadays in the hands of the "sound designer" and his computerized wizardry. But on Broadway, it is routine for tiny computer "mikes" to be tucked into hairdos, coat collars, and neckties. Most community theatres and schools will not have access to miniaturized mikes and surround sound due to limited budgets.

The alternative requires some thought, which may not have been the case in one high school where the orchestra leader passed a hand-mike to the singers each time they did a solo. The sight of Curly and Laurie singing "People Will Say We're in Love" while passing a mike back and forth is not to be believed.

In any event, we should carefully consider the staging of musical numbers in a production. It is no longer adequate only to use whatever directions are given in the existing script and adopt a kind of complacent attitude that implies, "Well, that's what the book says!"

Audiences have become accustomed, through the media, MTV, and rock concerts, to overwhelming spectacle. How does the staged musical compete with all this razzmatazz? The answer: it probably cannot, not directly.

What you can do is re-think the meaning, intention, and character of your musical numbers. In a recent production of Gilbert and Sullivan's *The Mikado,* all the old semicircles of chorus numbers and all those kimonos, or bathrobes, were thrown out. The production was fashioned as a musical comedy.

The "little girls from school" weren't docile and submissive but spirited, dancing liberated women. "Braid the Raven Hair" was transformed into a teaching lesson for Yum-Yum, with instruction in how to manage her husband-to-be. Nicholas Hytner transformed *Carousel* by making it a more realistic portrayal of life in a nineteenth-century mill town, where people actually worked at the mill.

The composer and lyricist, sometimes in collaboration with the book writers, are charged with the job of seeking out those moments that are best, or better, illustrated with music. The placement of the song must be intrinsic to the story and, as previously stated, a moment of intense meaning in the lives of the characters. The moments may, of course, be very comic as well as serious or dramatic. When a particular song doesn't work—according to the out-of-town critics and audience reactions—it is often instantly replaced.

A change of song also means that the script writer will have to alter dialogue to accommodate a new idea. Legendary in show business was a production called *Home, Sweet Homer* (based on the Greek *Odyssey*). It played the "road" outside New York for nearly a year and despite almost daily revisions it closed after one performance in New York City.

Don't be afraid to tinker with the number of singers. Even though your script indicates "a chorus number," consider whether it can be better staged with a quartet or a different combination of actors.

Defining the Show Songs

Dr. Doric Alviani, who taught at the University of Massachusetts, defined musical incidents in shows as atmosphere songs, character songs, plot songs, and the rarely used soliloquy. Encouraging his students to investigate the musical's structure in these terms enabled them to relate to these musical incidents in a less superficial way. Applying these apt and insightful definitions of musical expressions provides the director with a profoundly different way of approaching the staging of musical numbers. When this concept is embraced, even if the formula idea is objectively valid, then the presentation of a song, even when it is comic, is arrived at with respect.

There is a video entitled *The Best of Broadway Musicals,* taken from the *Ed Sullivan Show,* which features Celeste Holm singing "I'm Just a Girl Who Can't Say 'No'," from *Oklahoma!* This talented barely moves and hardly shifts her gaze, but so completely does she project the character and personality of Ado Annie that one learns more from this brief encounter than hours of discussion would reveal.

Should you decide to produce and/or direct one of the more typical musical comedies, such as *Anything Goes,* you may not find the well-integrated musical number we find in later classic musicals. All the more reason then to create your staging with a stylistic integrity in keeping with the time, place, and action.

Let's consider the five major song types.

The Atmosphere Song

This song provides us with a sense of place. One might recognize a debt to Aristotle and his requirements of the unities of time, place, and action. The most recognizable example of this type of song is certainly the opening number in *Oklahoma!* When Curly sings "Oh! What A Beautiful Morning!" we are transported to a time of day, place, and a historical period, with the additional "atmosphere" of weather.

Atmosphere songs tend to be the ones that open a show. They might, of course, easily be called atmosphere numbers, since they may not always have lyrics. *Carousel,* for example, creates the New England time, place, and period through an elaborate amusement park pantomime. A New York City mood and style is set by the almost choreographic opening of *Guys and Dolls.* Likewise, *My Fair Lady* has an overture that leads directly into a Covent Garden night scene, in the rain.

More typically, shows such as *Brigadoon, Annie Get Your Gun, Hello, Dolly, Showboat, A Funny Thing Happened on the Way to the Forum,* and *Bye Bye Birdie* have classic atmosphere songs. They offer the director a way to establish a sense of a show's style and concept through costumes, movement or action, and settings. If, for instance, you opt for a unit setting for *Oliver, Irma La Douce,* or *Kiss Me Kate,* your staging of an opening atmosphere song helps transport the audience to a desired place. And, except for *Oklahoma!,* these initial scene-setters present opportunities to stage good crowd scenes.

We can be grateful to Gilbert and Sullivan for the prototype atmosphere songs of

The Mikado ("We Are Gentlemen of Japan"), *H.M.S. Pinafore* ("We Sail the Ocean Blue"), and most of their operettas.

Your staging for an opening atmosphere song ought to be imaginative enough to captivate and convince the audience of the desired ambience of your chosen style. The subtlety of an opening atmosphere song is challenging to stage. You want to awaken a "Wow! this is going to be great!" feeling that is, at the same time, not so overwhelming that you are unable to recreate such excitement, action, and pizzazz again all evening. It has happened. So, leave some room for improvement.

An opening atmosphere song itself presents an opportunity to be inventive, relatively unhampered as yet by dictates of the plot to come. *Guys and Dolls* and *Carousel* offer rich possibilities for the inventive, thoughtful director. The witty, flippant beginning of *Kiss Me Kate,* "We Open in Venice," is a gold mine for audience involvement in jokes and asides. It is and isn't Shakespeare; it's show business!

The Character Song

This song is certainly the one most used in American musicals. A complete listing of them would be chapters, if not a book, by themselves.

A character song is one whose primary intention is to help us become acquainted with the personality, dreams, hopes, fears, and even torments of a lead role. The character song may occur anywhere in the script, and it may sometimes show psychological changes in a character. "Rose's Turn," from *Gypsy,* is an outstanding example of this happening very late in the show.

A character song must:

- Inform us about this individual.

- Develop understanding of this individual.

- Establish empathy, sympathy, or dislike of the individual.

- Instruct us how to react to, or what to expect from, this individual.

- Plan information for future reference to this person.

It should be immediately understood that physical presentation of the character song is vitally important. A good number of musicals have been produced that seem mistakenly to expect that simply delivering a number will magically, through the clever lyrics, suffice or at least fulfill an imagined purpose. Most of these songs demand the complete absorption of their meaning and projection of their ideas through the voice

AND body. Imagine an Annie singing "Tomorrow" with arms and hands flat at her sides and feet primly together. Where is the hope and relentless insistence on a better day she knows she will have?

Imagine Lorelie Lee singing "Diamonds Are a Girl's Best Friend" without showing us the glamor and glitter of those rocks as Marilyn Monroe did with such abandon in the film version of *Gentlemen Prefer Blondes.* Can Eliza Doolittle possibly project "Wouldn't It Be Loverly" without also being the vulnerable, wistful waif shivering in the rain of Covent Garden?

As a guide to better direction of the character song, here are two explicit examples of presentations that have been witnessed too many times.

The first is that of the singer/actor who really does have great vocal ability and is maybe even a musical comedy belter. You know the type: a big voice; a huge, expansive personality; and sometimes a physique to match. Confident that everyone is going to be dazzled by a grand vocal instrument, this actor simply stands there and sings— good and loud! But without body reactions and physical expression using arms, feet, hands, and face, the audience isn't carried further into the purpose of the song or the character singing it. Did this performance stop the show? The show stopped to let the audience listen to the singer, rather than continuing to flow toward meaning. Not good, even when the voice is good.

The second type is the eager, but usually novice, singer/actor who throws everything at us. Arms flailing, pacing rapidly to and fro with facial expressions in constant grimace, this actor is really "into" the number and wants us to know it. It's a presentation that screams frantically, "Showstopper!" The audience stops paying attention to a complete line of action and intent in order to once again be dazzled by "footwork."

Think for a moment of ballet or dance. Notice that ballet classes are always conducted in front of immense mirrors. Working before them brings an awareness of one's body: its alignment, its action of turning, and, certainly, its relationship to other bodies. One technique that has worked successfully is holding early musical show rehearsals in a ballet studio. It automatically makes the actors see themselves. The same could be accomplished with videotaping, but review would add hours to the rehearsal process.

The actor might also be encouraged to go home and "work out" (also known as "woodshedding") before home mirrors. The actor should constantly ask, "Is my body telling the story of my song precisely and effectively?"

Two gestures to avoid are those labelled by author Boland as the "side flail" and the "chest clutch." In the former, the actor simply raises or lowers arms and hands to the sides creating a windmill effect. It is totally unnatural. (See figs. 15.1 and 15.2.) In the latter, the actor constantly clutches one hand, or both, believing it soulful, when in reality it is just pathetic. Also, two hands raised open to the front over and over again makes the actor look nervous and serves no purpose. (See figs. 15.3 and 15.4.)

Fig. 15.1. Do this.

Fig. 15.2. Don't do the side flail.

Fig. 15.3. Do this.

Fig. 15.4. Don't do the chest clutch.

Fortunately, there are ways to overcome some of these unmotivated uses of gesture. One technique is having the actor think of the movement as a positive action. The actor would think, "Gesturing, using the body to help implement and compliment the emotions I am experiencing as I sing, is an offering from me, the character, to the people sensing and wanting to share these emotions." What is the typical way of offering something? An open hand, a forward thrust, directly in front of you.

From where does an offering emanate? The heart. A standard thought in song presentation ought to be that gestures pass through the front of the body—or heart—and not flap up and down at one's sides. A lesson on the use of gestures is to be learned from classical ballet where nearly all communication is from the upper body.

Character songs may not always be sung alone. Often, other characters can be used well as foils for or recipients of the action. "The Girl That I Marry" from *Annie Get Your Gun* and "Anything You Can Do" from the same show are examples.

Some classic character songs are

- "A Cockeyed Optimist," from *South Pacific*
- "Adelaide's Lament," from *Guys and Dolls*
- "Wouldn't It Be Loverly," from *My Fair Lady*
- "C'est Moi," from *Camelot*
- "Nothing" and "I Can Do That," from *A Chorus Line*
- "Sometimes Over the Rainbow"from *The Wizard of Oz*
- "Soon As I Get Home," from *The Wiz*
- "If I Were a Rich Man," from *Fiddler on the Roof*
- "I Am What I Am," from *La Cage Aux Folles*
- "Once You Lose Your Heart," from *Me and My Girl*
- "Some Enchanted Evening," from *South Pacific*
- "I Just Want to be a Star," from *Nunsense*

There are literally dozens of others in the vast repertory of American musicals. The point is this: give careful consideration to how you will stage the character song to best reveal the nuances of personality it suggests.

Directors have been heard to say, "Oh! This number is so well-known [or 'powerful'] that it doesn't need anything—just sing it!" That's wrong thinking. Though many songs are exquisite in their own right, they deserve a careful, thoughtful presentation, if only to do them justice. Through the skillfully staged character song, the audience becomes deeply involved in the hopes, dreams, determinations, and probable behavior of a character.

The Plot Song

The basis for this song is the skeleton of the show, those plot elements that define "the well-made play." This concept—that a play could be, or should be, based upon a carefully crafted formula—first occurred in the early eighteenth century. Victorien Sardou advocated a meticulous process that was later enlarged by Eugene Scribe. It was, in its time, another example of science and art running parallel in purpose. The "pièce bien faite," or "well-made play" has long had advocates and denouncers. The concept influenced Henrik Ibsen and G.B. Shaw.

The formula upon which a play may be built consists of

1. Exposition—things from the past

2. Preparation—the past explained and planted for the future

3. Complication—details added to create suspense

4. Suspense—concerns raised over conflicts

5. Conflict—tensions leading to a crisis

6. Crisis—concerns and tensions leading to a climax

7. Climax—series of crises needing to be solved have come to a peak

8. Outcome—all previous events have reached a resolution

A musical may have all of these elements arranged in different order. A musical may not have all of these elements, but it must have some of them, or there is no drama. The ideal song in a musical would reveal something about a character, advance the plot, and entertain.

"If I Loved You," from *Carousel,* might be considered a love song designed to introduce Billy Bigelow and Julie Jordan in a somewhat charming way. It does this indeed, but it is also the principal means of propelling the plot and establishing the depth of situation necessary to build the rest of the production.

Plot songs require careful staging in order to achieve their purpose. Too much choreography or too much spectacle may obscure the story line from being clearly stated. In one production of *Brigadoon,* the director thought the music to "Almost Like

Being in Love" was danceable. A boy and girl dance chorus was placed behind Fiona and Tommy. It thoroughly obscured the plot motive of the number.

The very charming song "Maria," from *The Sound of Music,* is essential to the audience understanding that Maria would be a less than satisfactory nun, thereby setting the conditions (preparation and complication) for the audience to accept her defection. It is essentially a plot device. This is also true in *Les Misérables.* Every song propels a long and complex story forward.

The modern musical has avoided the blatant formula but not the ingredients. Some musical settings create and solidify reasons for love and romance. While these songs fulfill our deep-seated desire for falling in love and sharing existence, the director recognizes them as serving a need within the structure of the script. They are more than evokers of a furtive tear. The staging of the plot song must be approached from something more than a "production number" attitude. Studiously note each factor in the song lyric that will convey information generating suspense or expectation of a future event.

The Soliloquy

This is the rare but special number that reveals a character's innermost thoughts. Not necessarily the first of such, but the most emphatic, was Billy Bigelow's soliloquy in *Carousel.* Like Shakespeare's Hamlet and Macbeth, Billy contemplates his future in order to change it.

Are the character song and the soliloquy different? Don't they accomplish the same purpose? Again, an analogy with Shakespeare is relevant. Every line of Shakespearean dialogue reveals new insights into the characters' behavior, principles, and outward appearances. But only in soliloquies, such as that of Hamlet, Macbeth, and Lady Macbeth, do we enter into the private mind of the individual and become either attracted or repulsed by his rationale. Soliloquy, as defined by Webster, is "a speech in a drama in which a character discloses innermost thoughts."

Sometimes in viewing a musical production, one has the feeling that the songs occur almost as interruptions to the "play." This often happens if the director tends to treat them as "numbers" rather than implements vital to the story. In a musical—as in any play, really—everything must lead up to the song moment, evoke it, and support it. The song must then blend all the rest of the scene, or play, together.

As rare as the soliloquy is, it serves to alert us to the pressing need to make the musical number work for the musical. Try to imagine *Showboat* without "Old Man River." Perhaps more of our best-loved songs, such as "Tomorrow" from *Annie* or "If I Were a Rich Man" from *Fiddler on the Roof,* ought to have the status of soliloquies.

The Tempo Song

In the current Broadway musical *Victor Victoria* there is a show-stopping number called "All that Jazz." Some authors refer to the ancestry of this musical piece as the Le Jazz Hot tempo song. Once very popular, even necessary to early musical comedies, the tempo song is an upbeat, lively, highly rhythmic and very danceable number. George Gershwin's "I Got Rhythm" and "Fascinatin' Rhythm" were typically used for tap dancing chorus numbers. In modern revues and biographical musicals, the tempo song is once again popular but in musical plays they have largely been absorbed into the plot, for example "June Is Bustin' Out All Over" from Rodgers and Hammerstein's *Carousel*.

Chapter 16
Choreography

In the Greek play *The Bacchae,* Dionysus summons the chorus to "Beat on your timbrels, make the strange wild music." Such a command must certainly have evoked some sort of patterned movement from the chorus representing Dionysus's female worshippers.

Choreography is the art of composing and arranging dances. That dancing is the creation of rhythmic and patterned bodily movements that are pleasant or rewarding to look at. By definition then, choreography and dancing would almost seem to be a single art. The fact is that for school and community musicals they *are* separable and may have very different impacts on a production. How is this possible?

There are ballet teachers—exceptionally able dancers themselves—who are very capable in a studio setting. Yet in their choreography for a show will lack relevance, coherence, and meaning in the context of the production. In contrast, there have been high school musicals where earnest students have quite naively put together production dancing that was outstanding. Good dancing cannot make inappropriate or irrelevant choreography suitable to a production. Good choreography thoughtfully developed through a story line may make untrained actors look nearly professional.

Dancing Adds Meaning

Ever since Agnes de Mille astounded the Broadway show world with her use of classical ballet and modern dance, we have been acutely aware how some aspects of the play story may be told in dance. The first thing the director should do when considering dance production numbers is question how they may be used to enhance the show's meaning. The test questions are

1. How can I make this dance tell a story to the audience?

2. How can I make the audience relate this dance to the play they are watching?

If there is one area or characteristic of the amateur musical that is apt to suffer in comparison to professional shows, it is the dance numbers. Broadway dancers are highly trained and extraordinarily skilled performers. They are prepared for the rigorous and complex choreography demanded by competitive show business. The choreographers, or dance arrangers, are inventive. More often than not they have been "boys" and "girls" in the chorus and are well schooled in what the dancer can and must do.

Most amateur productions simply cannot assemble enough safely trained and talented dancers to duplicate a truly professional chorus. In some nonprofessional musicals, dance steps look awkward or are executed in a very mechanical, self-conscious way. The choreography "made up" for them may not seem to grow naturally out of the events on stage and is therefore just a lot of nonrelevant footwork. It might serve your show better just to leave out a complicated number. If you have suffered through awful Highland flings in amateur *Brigadoons* or jerky Charlestons in *The Boy Friend,* you will appreciate the suggestion to consider very carefully the dance numbers.

Early in the process of staging your musical, you need to get together for a long, l-o-n-g, musical session with the musical director and the orchestra conductor. If you do not happen to be a musician yourself, these people can point out clues in the score, pieces of melody, rhythm, or tempo that will give a choreographer a richer feeling for the action of the music.

The choreographer also may be helped by audio recordings or videos to recognize where musical phrases change and how the show's motifs are involved in the dance. A familiar tune, ballad, or love song, reinforced by the dance movements on stage, adds deeper meaning to the production. Choreography needs to respond to the syncopated, energetic tempos and orchestral effects that have become the trademark of the modern musical.

Once upon a time in the Broadway musical, dancing was viewed primarily as having a "show-stopper" purpose. Long lines of tap dancing choruses were standard. Whole shows, such as *42nd Street,* were written about the chorus girl who becomes a "star." *Oklahoma!* transformed all of that, as did the jazz-style choreography of Jack Cole. Nothing has ever been the same. The more recent *A Chorus Line* makes the integral part a dancer plays in professional theatre strikingly clear.

Susan Stroman's exciting and entertaining choreography for *Crazy for You* and *Showboat* has a spirit and energy that is both witty and electrifying, serving the character of these productions perfectly. It would be hard to think of any performance of these works without dancing of this caliber.

Looking Good!

How, then, does the amateur production meet a comparable level of performance?

First of all, try to be thoroughly aware of the potential of your cast or performers, even before selecting a show. Don't sign off on rights to *A Chorus Line* unless you have well-trained dancers. Even when choosing *Carousel* or *Brigadoon,* work with a few actors to see what kinds of movement or athletic action looks good on them.

Select a choreographer—or train yourself—to be a teacher, guide, and theatrical personality who will be sensitive to amateurs who can be encouraged to do their best; and, as the wag exhorted when stopped in New York City and asked directions on how one gets to Carnegie Hall, "Practice! Practice! PRACTICE!"

Theme and Style

Think of dance numbers that relate to the show's inherent theme. Consider these examples: good guys versus bad guys; boys falling in love with girls; folks happy to be awake and alive; adorable orphans imitating or satirizing their "betters."

Instead of trying to create dazzling footwork, relate the dance to the chosen style of the production. Cockneys in *My Fair Lady* ought to be eccentric; miners in *Paint Your Wagon* and sailors in *Carousel* should be rowdy and earthy. Dance hall girls in *Sweet Charity* need to be sensual and sexual, yet not embarrassing. Strippers' "bumps and grinds" may be inappropriate to your cast, but deliberate, determined poses and strutting can be very funny.

One might even engage the school's math department in working out geometric routines (as for marching bands) that can be very effective for the large patterns of movement in big numbers. Covering a lot of ground (or stage area) in more or less intricate maneuvers gives an immediate feeling of action and can use up a lot of musical measures.

Relevant Dancing

Ask whether you can judiciously cut or shorten dance numbers without affecting the show's artistic quality and integrity. It's unusual for a musical's composer actually to have written out the dance music of a show. This task is most often given to a dance arranger skilled at the work, who will select the tunes and sections of a song, or musical setting, for a dance number. Sometimes the length of a number may have been dictated by the need to move or change scenery in a complicated professional production.

With proper attention to the music requirements, you can make the length of a dance more suited to your needs and the talent available. For example, if you don't have enough actors to accommodate the long "Entrance of the Siamese Children" in *The King and I,* have the actors march around twice. "Short and sweet" is often better than long and tedious.

A careful analysis and reading of the material in the libretto, comparing it with the score, will indicate why a dance is included. If the original Broadway actor had a special talent as a dancer, such as Ray Bolger or Gwen Verdon, a dance may have been created just for that personality. If your Dolly Gallagher Levi isn't a dancer, change the dance.

Essential or Atmosphere?

Many dances are integrated into the script and are an essential part of the story. Work hard on these. Others may be purely atmospheric or entertaining and will not suffer if you take some liberties in their presentation.

The Dream Ballet in *Oklahoma!* is a relatively easy piece to choreograph and stage, and you may freely use non-dancers as walk-ins. Less simple is the musical number that opens the show solely as a dance. *Guys and Dolls* comes to mind. We haven't yet met the characters, nor learned anything about the story and its period. The same is true of *Hello, Dolly.* Both of these, however, can be effectively staged not as dance numbers but as street scenes. Shoppers, panhandlers, newsboys, people going to and coming from work, policemen, and schoolchildren may all be used to simulate the ambience of a city, Times Square, or a small town without dancing. Opening numbers such as these can be made into natural scenes rather than overextended, unartful dances.

Authenticity

Should a dance number in a production such as *Brigadoon* be authentic? Yes and no. The Sword Dance by Harry Beaton ought to be as genuine as possible, given your actor's capabilities. Note, however, that the MacConnachy Square dances are free, lively expressions of the spirit of the townspeople, and that spirit should dominate without making a mockery of Highland dancing.

Let us suppose you plan to stage *Kiss Me Kate.* A traveling group of players—supposedly in Italy—are planning to "open in Venice." Here you are seemingly faced with two possibilities: use Italian Renaissance dance figures or English Shakespearean-style dancing. Authenticity, or accuracy, would be not quite correct here. The actors are modern, and this version of *The Taming of the Shrew* is contemporary; therefore, the dance numbers should be too.

Dance has come full circle in the Broadway musical, and we are once again in a period when jazzy, athletic, exuberant, and eccentric action is the style. If your *Kiss Me Kate* is for the 1990s, draw upon everything contemporary—be it rock and roll or line dancing. In this show, the entire plot and circumstances revolve around men being faithful to women and vice versa. This alone is a source of dance activity: men cruise indiscriminately and women flirt constantly; men strut; women preen. The choreography may shift attention from one to the other while creating movement between "Renaissance-like" geometric patterns of movement.

Do It Well

Much has been said, both in this text and other more definitive works, about the special theatrical nature of the American musical. Apart from the obvious fact that people sing, dance propels the story and sometimes heightens the dramatic effect. Therefore, dance, or dancing, in your production is a paramount feature that not only refines the production but defines its very nature. Above all, then, dance must be done expressively and well.

We strongly advise that you follow procedures outlined earlier in both the beginning reading rehearsals (Chapter 11) and initial staging rehearsals (Chapter 13).

The dancers must be carefully involved and integrated from the earliest explorations of your material. Don't, repeat *don't,* simply send the kids with a sense of rhythm and athletic potential off somewhere to learn a bunch of steps and then expect them to come "do their thing" at a later date. They must be involved in scenes at all times as part of the total ensemble. Nothing is as disturbing in any amateur play or musical as seeing a large variety of chorus or background people, who are supposed to be involved with the action onstage, who don't react to what is happening! Deadpan is deadly. Train your ensemble to listen, respond, and react in whatever manner a scene requires.

Chapter 17
Setting the Stage

The stage setting will be one of the most demanding facets of your "gem" of a show. The setting, simple or elaborate, is vital in conveying the time and place within which a scene is enacted.

Nothing about producing a musical show, or any play for that matter, is likely to be easy. Because this is an art form, discipline and effort are necessities. Good help is an asset. If you have an experienced designer (scenographer in today's theatre), the task is less stressful, simply because communication in theatre terms and purposes is more immediately understood.

Often, the musical show director takes on the function of the show's set designer through necessity. This is not a bad solution since, presumably, the director knows what is needed and wanted for the accomplishment of specific scenes. On the other hand, being both designer and director places tremendous demands on the director's time and temperament. Certainly the benefits of another's imagination and viewpoint would be welcome, especially the designer-artist who will think in terms that may escape others who are seeking a "practical" solution to scenic demands.

Inspiration

Whether working with a scenic designer or developing your own set designs, you will need to ask some questions about the material. Earlier we indicated that some musicals are brisk and jazzy (*Bye Bye Birdie*), others elegant (*My Fair Lady*), and some melodic and grand in scope (*The Student Prince* and *Camelot*). The descriptive adjectives employed to define or suggest a specific musical are varied and manifold. These may be the key to how you will provide the settings for your show. A primary purpose of the setting is to create an appropriate atmosphere where certain action by three-dimensional, moving actors can take place. The setting should clearly establish a time and place—reinforcing what the play is saying. Don't hesitate to go to picture sources in libraries or museums for inspiration.

Technical and/or mechanical requirements ought to be listed and discussed at the beginning of the process. The musical, more so than legitimate plays (Shakespeare aside), requires multiple settings. Shifting locales, scenes within scenes, simultaneous scenes, and even moving panoramic scenes can all be found in music theatre scripts. Most modern stages in professional theatres have been designed to make scene shifts practical. Most school auditoriums and community theatres have not. Flying space, trapdoors, and adequate wing spaces are easy marks when the building committee must cut the budget and shunts them aside as "frills." You must therefore carefully consider the possibilities and limitations of your stage. Ask

- What are the dimensions of your stage?

- What equipment does your stage have for flying or moving sets?

- Is there space to use moveables, such as wagons?

In community theatre, schools, and colleges, it is often considered "clever" to *see* the crew scurrying around the stage changing sets and props. Most of the time this is very unprofessional and implies a lack of good old-fashioned imagination. Remember that shapes, outlines, and architectural suggestions are all effective means for helping the audience realize the content of a scene.

Overdoing

> Generally speaking, amateur theatre presentations err on the side of too much scenery, rather than too little.

This may seem a philistine attitude given the fact that scenic design budgets for the contemporary Broadway production may easily be in excess of two, three, or five-million dollars. When we experience the artistic and mechanical wonders of a *Sunset Boulevard, Showboat,* or *Phantom of the Opera,* it is easy to see why this is so. The amateur theatre seeking to duplicate, or at least approach, the razzle-dazzle of Broadway, television, or movie technology is vulnerable. One need not, however, be intimidated by Broadway technology and money—be challenged instead.

A setting that sprawls all across your stage space and takes long minutes to change may be impressive, but won't aid your production's pace and style. Salzburg, Austria may be extraordinarily scenic and surrounded by mountains, but a rock or tree stump and effective tree branches say more about Maria's contemplative mood in the opening song in *The Sound of Music*.

A few popular musicals are remarkable in requiring only one scenic setting. Shows such as *Man of La Mancha, The Fantasticks, Roar of the Greasepaint, Smell of the Crowd, A Funny Thing Happened on the Way to the Forum*, and *Something's Afoot* (a murder-mystery musical) can be designed as one-set productions with slight additional elements. *Oliver, Company, A Chorus Line, Pippin*, and *Once upon a Mattress* are also easily adapted to the single setting treatment.

Nevertheless, multiple scenes are still the norm for most musicals. *Brigadoon* shifts rapidly from Scotland in the eighteenth century to New York City in the twentieth, even requiring some simultaneous effects. Physical methods for achieving these effects have been used for centuries. Excellent texts, both historical and technical, exist as guides.

The Aesthetics

A school director reported that he went to see a new Broadway production five or six times just so he could studiously make dozens of thumbnail sketches of the sets and costumes. Back in his hotel room, he would complete and color them. He explained, "My productions were almost an exact copy of the originals!" One has to admire his determination, if nothing else.

Determination may not be a good substitute for imagination. The director described above is missing an important aspect. Each of us wishes that our productions could be unique to ourselves and our performers. Part of the goal of the school production is to teach creativity and aesthetic resourcefulness. In community theatre we strive for accomplishment, entertainment, and professionalism without being excessive or imitative.

The first and most basic lesson of aesthetic philosophy is that each and every work of art—regardless of its time and place—must have singular and original objectives special only to itself.

Basic Approaches

For thinking your problems through and making considered judgements in staging, think of the following thirteen basic approaches as solutions to the multiple scene problem. They are workable and cost effective. The once-popular artistic phrase "less is more" is suitable for today's school and community productions. Make your settings as attractive as possible but not so elaborate that they detract from the action and distract the audience with extensive scene changes and long pauses.

Here are thirteen basic approaches.

- The Box Set
- The Trip Set
- The Trip and Fly Set
- The Wagon Set
- The Jackknife Set
- The Revolve Set
- The Double Revolve Set

- The Ramp and Level Set
- The Unit Set
- The Simultaneous Set
- The Drop Set(s)
- Any combination of these sets
- The Photo/Slide Projection Set

Following is a brief description and an illustration of each, along with some suggestions for specific uses. The illustrations imply the use of standard flats or set pieces and low levels on casters.

A box set (fig. 17.1) is a three-sided arrangement of standard flats, or hard surfaces, that form a "room" with the "fourth wall" toward the audience. The view from above gives the name to the structure.

A trip set (fig. 17.2) may be two or more hinged flats or surfaces that can fold in on themselves for easy removal or change. In European theatre this is also called a "book" style.

A trip and fly set (fig. 17.3) is only possible where there is some kind of overhead flying space or facility for raising and lowering scenery. The concept may be useful to consider for small overhead backgrounds.

The wagon set (fig. 17.4) refers to any arrangement of flats, set pieces, or props placed on a low level equipped with casters, or wheels, for easy rolling on or off stage. Without tracks in the floor, as in Broadway theatres, you may need a pull-rope or push-stick. Caution: fiber, plastic, or any non-metal casters are best on moveable wagons or levels.

A jackknife set (fig. 17.5) was devised for stages having very little backstage space

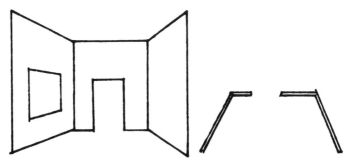

Fig. 17.1. The box set.

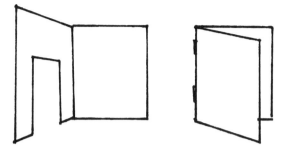

Fig. 17.2. The trip set.

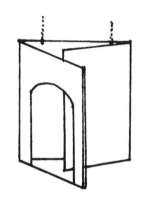

Fig. 17.3. The trip and fly set.

Fig. 17.4. The wagon set.

or limited depth. Its obvious problem is one of "masking," or being able to hide or cover it when it is off-stage. One corner is usually stationary.

A revolve set (fig. 17.6), or turntable, is a simple method for making quick changes of smaller set pieces. Large turntables are excellent but require lots of mechanical construction and an anchor point in the stage floor. Small levels can be turned and need not be circular in shape.

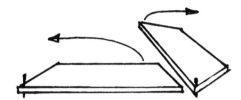

Fig. 17.5. The jackknife set.

A double revolve (fig. 17.7) greatly multiplies the possible scenic combinations. Once again, however, it necessitates accurate construction and the ability to maneuver gracefully or unobtrusively.

The ramp and level set (fig. 17.8) is an arrangement of various heights, stairs, and inclined surfaces that can suggest different locales by changing furniture, props, or flats. This set works wonderfully if you can also fly scenic pieces or use trip methods.

The unit set (fig. 17.9) is so named because ONE arrangement may be used effectively for many different purposes.

The simultaneous set (fig. 17.10) implies two different areas at the same time. It is most often used to create an indoor-outdoor scene but can be used imaginatively for many other requirements.

The drop set (fig. 17.11) is certainly the most popular one for musicals, because it leaves lots of room for action or choreography. The "drop" is any large painted cloth hung behind the actors. A drop may also be a cut-drop that permits movement through the drop or from upstage to downstage.

Combining the practical uses or concepts of any of these arrangements offers nearly unlimited possibilities for solving scenic problems. Perhaps you can make use of a small unit setting combined with wagons or a small backdrop or trip set.

A projection set makes use of some form of photo-assisted design or structure. As

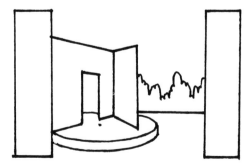

Fig. 17.6. The revolve set.

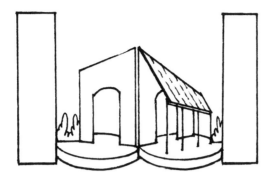

Fig. 17.7. The double revolve set.

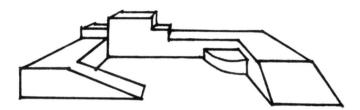

Fig. 17.8. The ramp and level set.

Fig. 17.9. The unit set.

early as the 1920s, theatre artists experimented with slide projections, painted glass slides, and dye-painted transparencies in Linnebach projectors. The results were not always workable theatrically but were artistically exciting. The obvious drawbacks were diffused images competing with the stage light needed on the actors. As better machinery developed, projection became a true art form. Photo negatives, colored gel, and Gobo projections (with appropriate lighting instruments) held many suggestive and decorative possibilities.

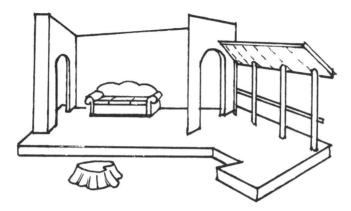

Fig. 17.10. The simultaneous set.

Computer-assisted imagery has further transformed projected scenic design. Super-sized TV screen technology has given designers video capabilities that are almost unlimited. Video animation techniques on a massive scale are commonplace in rock shows and Las Vegas panoramic spectacles, as well as in theme parks.

The theatre industry has also created special lighting instruments such as Pani projectors, cyberlights, and intellabeams that can be utilized with laser technology, effectively eliminating previous problems with intensity and illumination. The problem now is one of cost.

It is hard to imagine that projection devices will become commonplace in schools and community theatres in the near future. Rear projection screens and inventive designers can perform miracles, however.

Two fundamental problems occur with any projected scenery:

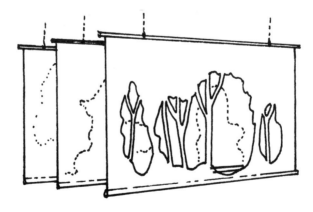

Fig. 17.11. The drop set(s).

1. A projection needs darkness to be visually effective, but in most musicals we need lots of stage light on singers/dancers. Ways to overcome this built-in restriction are extremely expensive requiring special screen material or superprojectors.

2. Front projection is required in small stage spaces, and this results in actors throwing shadows. This effect of moving shadows, however, can be of great advantage in choreography or modern dance.

We might have included a fourteenth approach, involving the use of scenic flats—the common wood-frame and canvas-covered unit that is standard in the theatre. The new term "Hollywood flat" refers to a wooden frame with a hard cover, such as Luan or plywood, that is now widely used in television. Flats can be made transparent, semi-opaque, veloured, brocaded, or even double-sided.

The history of flats and their evolution is a fascinating study in itself. During the Italian Renaissance, for example, flats were placed in horizontal tracks on the stage floor to permit movement left and right, in and out, and create new spaces and effects. The technique was used in the 1994–1995 Tony-winning show *Smokey Joe's Cafe,* designed by Heidi Landesman. Nothing goes out of style in the theatre if you apply imagination.

The theatre's acknowledged master of scenic projection is Joseph Svoboda of Czechoslovakia. His designs for opera, ballet, and stage plays are worthy of extensive study.

Suggestions for Using the Basic Approaches

- Mt. Greylock Regional High School staged *Guys and Dolls* with a single setting and backdrop (fig. 17.12). Both the Mission and Hot Box units were flat frames that "tripped." Later, the Havana scene easily rolled on in front of the other units.

- For *Bye Bye, Birdie,* four wagon units built on four-by-four foot wagons could be turned and assembled in a number of combinations for the City Hall of Sweet Apple or the TV studio at The Ed Sullivan Theatre (figs 17.13 and 17.14).

- *She Loves Me* is easily designed as a single revolve for the Shop and the Street, with wagons for the Apartment and Restaurant.

- *The Fantasticks,* of course, always works well in a Unit Set, as does *Roar of the Greasepaint, the Smell of the Crowd.*

- Combine a wagon (or two) with drops for Henry Higgins's Study, and you have an efficient, effective *My Fair Lady.*

- *Two Gentlemen of Verona,* the rock musical, lends itself to a unit set (fig. 17.15).

- *Oh! What a Lovely War!* is a ramp and level set designed by Sam Slack (fig. 17.16).

Fig. 17.12. Mt. Greylock Regional High School design for *Guys and Dolls*.

Fig. 17.13. Wagon units, *Bye Bye Birdie*, Mt. Greylock Regional High School.

Fig. 17.14. Wagon units, *Bye Bye Birdie*.

Fig. 17.15. Unit set, *Two Gentlemen of Verona*, Berkshire Community College.

Fig. 17.16. Ramp and level set, *Oh! What a Lovely War!* Design by Sam Slack.

Arena Staging

Arena staging is familiar to anyone who has visited a summer tent show or music circus presentation. The audience is seated on at least three sides, four-side seating being the norm (fig. 17.17). The arena offers innovative possibilities, and not just a few difficulties, but is a wonderful experience for the audience and a terrific challenge for actors, dancers, and singers. An arena staging places the action of the play in the center of a larger area. It need not be in the round to work well.

In arena staging, exits and entrances are made right through the audience aisles, providing extra humorous possibilities or intimacy for moments of empathy. The action of singers and dancers moving in and out while "in character" adds an additional dimension of entertainment and not a few unpredictable events. During a production of *My Fair Lady,* Henry Higgins made his entrance to sing "I've Grown Accustomed to Her Face," when an elderly patron rose and engaged him in conversation, finally asking for directions to the rest room. *Candide* was done on Broadway environmentally, in the round, with great effect. Any Gilbert and Sullivan work lends itself to arena staging, as does *The Boy Friend.*

Arena staging has the great advantage of requiring less scenery but demands efficient imagination in using what is available. Where to place the musicians may be a problem for cooperative deliberations among the stage and musical directors and orchestra conductor.

A special role has been assigned to the scenic designer in modern theatre. Embracing all the arts, the designer is in a position to make contributions to theatre that

Fig. 17.17. Arena staging, *The Music Man,* Town Players of Pittsfield, Massachusetts.

may not have even been a part of the playwright's vision. The set designer is both a craftsman and an artist. Discuss with the scenic designer how the imaginary matter (air) of stage space may be sculpted and formed to illuminate the production. Where the script suggests a jail, perhaps only a cell window need be used. A garden can be evoked by leaf patterns spontaneously falling on a backdrop and a garden bench.

List of Suppliers

There are a number of companies throughout the United States that rent painted drops. Specialty drops are available from the following:

Scenery

Fullerton Light Opera Co., Inc.
218 W. Commonwealth Avenue
Fullerton, CA 92632

Grosh Scenic
4114 Sunset Blvd.
Hollywood, CA 90029

Joseph C. Hansen Co.
423 W. 43rd Street
New York, NY 10036

Charles H. Stewart Co.
P.O. Box 187
Somerville, MA 02114

Pittsburgh Civic Light Opera
719 Liberty Avenue
Pittsburgh, PA 15222

Tobins Lake Studio
7030 Old U.S. 23
Brighton, MI 48116

Schell Scenic Studio
841-843 S. Front Street
Columbus, OH 43206

Scenic Materials, Hardware, and Paint

CBS Television Plastic Designs
535 West 56th Street
New York, NY 10019

Mikan Theatricals
86 Tide Mill Road
Hampton, NH 03842

Flex Moulding, Inc.
16 East Lafayette Street
Hackensack, NJ 07601

Mutual Hardware Corp.
5-45 49th Avenue
Long Island City, NY 11101

Set and Prop Rental

The Design Group
Big Top Balloons
8616 Xylon Avenue N.
Brooklyn Park, MN 55445

Projection Screen

Da-Lite Screen Co.
P.O. Box 137
Warsaw, IN 46581

Using Color

In scenic design color is not an absolute; there are no rules that can meet the requirements of mood and style in every stage setting. At the same time, most school and community theatre productions need to be aware of some standard ideas and associations we have about color, since they may be required to use color sparingly or for more immediate impact.

Most off-off-off Broadway productions are not going to have either the budget or the personnel to duplicate the scenic effects of today's mega shows. That doesn't mean that they need to be any less tasteful, atmospheric, or visually pleasing, however. A little well-intentioned color goes a long way. Your school art department, graphic designer, or community commercial artist could be a great help with color practices.

> It is vital to think at the outset that you will have three different color media to work with and, consequently, three palettes of color all affecting one another. They are settings, costumes, and lighting.

Most directors must rely on others to assist in settings, costumes, and lighting, but having the ability to communicate some of your thoughts will avoid serious mistakes. Let's concentrate on color in the scenic design at this point.

Color's uniqueness is that it consists of a trinity of itself. Color is hue, value, and intensity. Hue means red, blue, or whatever. Value is the degree of greyness. Intensity is brightness. These elements are generally used or applied in a highly personal, subjective way and could only be discussed at length in a different text. We can affirm, however, that the director needs to work very closely with these elements in designing lights, costumes, and sets.

General Principles

Warmer colors in the red, orange, and yellow spectrums tend to advance in the visual field. Thus, large areas can be made intimate when painted warmly. Cooler colors in the blue, green, and violet spectrums tend to move further away or suggest distance. Spaciousness can be achieved, even in a small area, with these colors. If the stage is small, use cool colors upstage and warm downstage. It will look bigger.

The mirth and lightheartedness of comedies has generally been best expressed in the brighter and warmer color ranges. The serious or somber mood is most often captured in the cooler colors. Color produces an emphatic psychological response in nearly all human beings, with some allowances made for cultural backgrounds.

Red is excitable, physical, passionate, suggesting violence in *Macbeth,* but can be elegant and aristocratic in *Hello, Dolly.* Yellow is sunshine, light, and knowledge. Orange, the splendid mixture of red and yellow, is a proud, ostentatious, and sometimes opinionated color.

Blue, in its purest forms, may also be aristocratic, because it is so austere and deep like the ocean or the zenith of the sky. Green, the blue and yellow combination, is supposed to be restful and calming. It implies springtime, young growth, and pleasant things to come. It is the toughest or riskiest color on stage, however, due to its effects on lighting. Violet, or purple, the most elusive color in the wavelength, has traditionally been used to suggest royalty, religion, and authority. It is, in short, the color of wealth. Gold also implies strength and power.

No matter how you use color to create your setting, keep in mind that harmony of tones, hues, and values must be a prime goal. Red or black on white is striking, but it is also distracting and confusing. Pure white is hardly ever used on stage. Under lights, it's simply too glaring.

A word about paint. Housepaint just doesn't work in theatre. The key word is "color." We often encounter the paint crew of a "local" production buying paint in the hardware store. While this is a convenience, it is probably a poor choice of product. The theatrical industry is so immense that somewhere someone offers a solution to almost any problem. Paint is no exception. (See the list of suppliers in this chapter.)

Scenic paint is manufactured by several companies that advertise extensively in theatre magazines. The time and effort taken to order and receive their paint is well worth the results. Most latex house paint formulated for the interior or exterior of a home is so heavily saturated with an opaque base, or tinted with white, that it reacts badly under stage lighting. Scenic paint should react to and reflect your lighting designer's mood settings. House paint gobbles up illumination and is flat, dull, and uninteresting. Be especially careful that you do not use a latex enamel. The glossy surface will reflect light in a most distracting way. Another drawback to the common paints found in a hardware or paint store is the thick film they create when dry. If you are using muslin or canvas, cloth-covered flats for your sets, ordinary paint will "alligator," or crack, after a few uses. House paint adds tremendous weight to your sets and makes them relatively useless in a short time.

True scenic paint, however, can be used to create endless effects of glazes, shadowing, or deep saturated color by overpainting dozens of times. It is available from the following suppliers:

Demand Products, Inc.
4620 South Atlanta Road
Atlanta, GA 30080

Dudley Theatrical
5088 Harley Drive
P.O. Box 519
Walkertown, NC 27051

Gothic Coatings, Inc.
1 Continental Hill
P.O. Box 189
Glen Cove, NY 11542

Mann Brothers
757 North La Brea Avenue
Hollywood, CA 90038

Sculpt or Coat
Nationwide Dealers
800-743-0379

ROSCO (Main Office)
36 Bush Avenue
Port Chester, NY 10573 (has franchised dealers)

Since costumes, because of the materials and fabrics, light differently than painted surfaces, study a few samples of both under lights to see how they react. Bear in mind that theatre lighting is an art unto itself. Do not make the assumption that mixing colors for the stage is anything similar to an artist mixing oil paints.

The scenic designer's painted elevation or the costume designer's palate can be such beguiling, appealing constructions in themselves that you can be misled. There have been many attempts at show "concepts" wherein having the sets and costumes the very same colors was thought to be clever or different. Usually, it is just distracting.

Color also may be used to make something ordinary into the extraordinary. An example involved the need to create a "castle wall" for the set of *Camelot*. When the director of a show at Pittsfield High School saw a four-cup carry container, he visualized several dozen glued together and painted gold and bronze becoming Arthur's Throne Room. Massing the forms created an effective three-dimensional surface that also had ornate doors with bottle caps added for medieval detail.

The Future

Computer technology has become an integral part of the theatre arts. Trade magazines and theatre industry services refer to computer-assisted design as CAD and computer-aided drafting as CADD when there are design capabilities. Software programs that aid in technical drawings as well as color renderings are available.

Designers are able to experiment with the three-dimensional structure by changing its location, frame of reference, or orientation at will. CAD programs automatically allow for the use of scale drawings, even in metrics or fractions. Zoom potential allows for an increase or reduction of size in any part of an object or a whole drawing. Three-dimensional settings in perspective are easily combined with figures for immediate visualization of images.

A more important use of computer technology is computer control and adaptation of lighting instruments incorporated into the scenic concept. Any kind of natural effect, be it rain, snow, volcanic eruption, or movement of clouds and water, can be accomplished by projection devices.

Laser projection is a routine experience for many of us, and is now extensively used by scenic designers. The equipment necessary, however, and the operational skills required place many of these techniques beyond the reach of most school and community theatres. Eventually, state of the art projected scenery, animatronics, and high power multimedia film effects may be available to us all.

According to the May 1995 issue of *Theatre Crafts Magazine,* an extraordinary extravaganza called EFX premiered at the MGM Grand Hotel and Casino in Las Vegas. On a stage 196 feet by 115 feet are 3,033 ellipsoidal reflector spotlights; 53 fresnels; 1,154 PAR cans; 229 striplights; 146 strobes; 336 automated luminaires; 7 followspots; and 225 miscellaneous luminaires, including 8 GAM scene machines (projectors), Pani projectors, and cyberlights for floating cloud effects.

Chapter 18
The Costumes

Individual creativity must exist in the cooperative enterprise of producing a theatrical event. The director oversees a vast number of individual, creative artists.

No individual work of art can be created democratically. For example, only one painter produced the *Mona Lisa*. The same is true for the work of theatre artists, including the costume designer. What makes the work of these artists unique is that they all contribute to the single goal of putting on a production.

Because all final decisions rest with the director, he or she needs to be qualified to make choices relating to all the other artists, including scenic design, lighting, and costume design.

It would be presumptuous to dictate how to costume a musical show in a single chapter. We must refer you to the bibliography, which lists a number of excellent texts on the subject of the special craft of costume design. We can give you some fundamentals, however.

It is very important to say very emphatically that a director cannot, and should not, change the work of the other artists involved without consultation and/or sufficient reason. A good director does not arbitrarily alter a set color or a lighting effect or order that a costume be changed. It simply is not done in the professional theatre, where contracts and unions safeguard the integrity and reputation of the theatre artist. If a costume—or anything else—strikes a wrong note, the director should consult that particular artist.

The Process

It would be ideal if one could engage a designer to make costumes for each production. The reality in amateur theatre, however, is that the director is faced with the necessity of either renting or assembling a wardrobe for a given production. Still, the principles of the art of costuming can be a reliable guide to the selection of costumes. What are some of the important aspects of professional costuming that might help you? A brief idea of the working methods of a professional designer is very instructive to a director's thinking processes.

A professional designer, after accepting a job through an agent or personal contact, begins with a thorough study of the script. Becoming familiar with the property is essential before any other discussions occur; this allows the designer to form some impressions of the characters and situations.

In the professional theatre, each designer is also responsible for a budget, and the following steps are absolutely essential:

1. A production conference is held with producer and director, and possibly other designers as well.

2. A conference is held with all designers present for discussion of an approach or concept. Will this production be historical (if so, will it be accurate?) or will it be stylized? What will the overall "look" be in terms of color, line, visual materials, and the like?

3. All the designers prepare preliminary sketches, usually in black and white, or simple pencil drawings responding to the previously discussed concept.

4. The costume designer will prepare a "costume plot," especially important for a musical (fig. 18.1). The plot will show exactly which characters are on stage together and how many costumes are ultimately required.

5. The preliminary drawings, often a series of comparative sketches two or three inches high, will emphasize the silhouette style of all the clothing. If "folk pattern" is a feature of the costumes, it is illustrated.

6. If everyone—designers and director—agree, the final process begins. In professional theatre, designs must actually be dated and signed and/or be notarized to avoid future misunderstandings.

7. The costume designer begins the final color plates, or drawings, that will be transformed into real clothes. As part of this designing process, the designer will select samples of actual materials and fabrics to be used. Note in the illustration (figs. 18.2 and 18.3) that swatches have been attached directly to the drawings.

8. Throughout the entire period of preparation, the designer will supervise all the cutting, fitting, and final construction or building of a costume.

9. The designer is usually responsible for the supervision of all accessories, wigs, and makeup, because they relate directly to the "look" of the character.

10. About a week before the inevitable dress rehearsal, the director schedules a "dress parade." In nonprofessional productions, this step is often overlooked

COSTUME PLOT				"ANY PRODUCTION"					

CHARACTER	11	12	13	14		21	22	23	24	TOTALS
NELLIE	TENNIS OUTFIT		STREET DRESS (RED)	OFFICE SUIT		ADD CAPE	SAME AS 11	BALL GOWN (WHITE)	SAME AS 23	4½ EST. $750.00
FRANK	BLUE SUIT	REPEAT	TUXEDO	SPORT SHIRT-SLACKS		GREY SUIT	REPEAT		TUXEDO	4 EST. $500.00
GLORIA		WAITRESS OUTFIT	HAT, COAT, ACCESS'RS	SAME AS 12			TENNIS DRESS		BALL GOWN	4 EST. $600.00
BILL	ARGYLE SWEATER SLACKS	REPEAT		TUXEDO			SPORT COAT SLACKS		TUXEDO	3 EST $500.00
GIRLS CHORUS	SPORT SHIRTS SKIRTS			STREET DRESS			SAME AS 11		BRIDESMAIDS	18 $4000.00
BOYS CHORUS	CREW SHIRTS SHORTS			STREET DRESS			SAME AS 11		FORMALS	18 $4000.00

Fig. 18.1. A typical costume plot.

in the frantic, last-minute, too-much-to-do atmosphere, but it can save many headaches. Try to get it in, even if it must occur during a regular rehearsal. There will still be time to make adjustments and changes.

Borrowing

Nonprofessional productions may not have the funds or personnel to create costumes from scratch. Fortunately, in some areas of the country, colleges with active theatre departments are very willing to loan costumes and sets to high schools and community theatres. The favor is returned, and many sets, costumes, and props are used reciprocally.

Borrowing entails certain responsibilities in addition to merely returning the item. A standard rule, and part of a professional attitude, is that one does not cut or alter other groups' materials, such as sets or costumes, without permission. Clothes may be fitted, shortened, or adapted, but not changed. When borrowing, do confirm whether or not there is a fee and if cleaning after use is required.

Devote special attention to types of fabrics and tasteful combinations of colors when borrowing. We often hear the costume chairperson exclaim, "Oh! Yes! Ado An-

Fig. 18.2. Costume plate, chorus of *The Mikado,* Town Players of Pittsfield.

nie would wear that!" But in this case, "that" may be a velvet or polyester that would not have been available in the time given in *Oklahoma!* Traditionally productions of *Carousel* have been costumed in stylish, richly decorated, form-fitting dresses and sailor suits worthy of *Vogue* magazine. Not until Nicholas Hytner's extraordinary 1994 London production did we see factory working girls and salt-drenched seamen correctly dressed to make us concentrate on the story and not the "picture look."

Fig. 18.3. Costume plate, chorus of *The Mikado,* Town Players of Pittsfield.

Renting

Renting from a reliable company is an option, but it also has its dangers. One usually must take what the company has in stock in the sizes needed. Some rental companies seem to feel that the more sequins and glitter a costume has, the better it is. Thus, in spite of the best efforts to create an integrated work of excellence, some costumes may not reflect the character and personality of the performers.

Study all the historical references on clothing and style in the local library in an effort to avoid this rental limitation. This is an excellent exercise for students in a school production. With copy machines for sharing found information, perhaps art students can get involved in learning about styles, customs, and history. It is, after all, our clothing that people see first. It is what an audience responds to immediately in their search for a sense of both the play and the character.

The following are some rental agencies:

ABC Costume Shop
195 NE 59th Street
Miami, FL 33137

All Dressed Up
150 South Water
Batavia, IL 60510

Broadway Costumes, Inc.
954 West Washington Blvd
Chicago, IL 60607

CTG Costume Center
Theatre Group
3301 E. 14th Street
Los Angeles, CA 90023

The Costume Consortium
1209 Logan
Denver, CO 80203

The Costume Collection
1501 Broadway, Ste. 2110
New York, NY 10036

Costume Armour
Mill Street
P.O. Box 85
Cornwall, NY 12518

Costume Architects, Inc.
1536 Monroe Drive
Atlanta, GA 30324

Costume Holiday House
3038 Hayes Avenue
Fremont, OH 43420

The Costumer, Inc.
1020-1030 Barrett St.
Schenectady, NY 12305

D.C. Theatrics
734-736 Main Street
Buffalo, NY 14202

Eaves-Brooks Costume Co.
2107 41st Avenue
Long Island City, NY 11101

Hooker-Howe Costume Co.
46-52 S. Main Street
P.O. Box 5098
Bradford, MA 01835

Landes Costume Co.
811 N. Capitol Ave.
Indianapolis, IN 46204

Tracy Costumes
86 Tide Mill Road
Hampton, NH 03842

Costuming Realities

There are some practical considerations apart from types and styles of costuming. Will the outfit be worn primarily by a member of the dance ensemble? Is it too tight to allow for a dancer's "lifts"? What about the type of material? Author Boland had the dubious college experience of lifting a girl dancer to his shoulders in a production number for *Hit The Deck*. The last minute switch to a taffeta skirt looked pretty, but the material was incredibly slippery. Up she went to one shoulder and right on down the other to the floor. Taffeta is noisy onstage as well.

If theatre is an art of empathic communication, and an art of seeing, we must also consider the relationship of the audience to stage picture. A costume designer's trained eye is invaluable. What may look good on the street (or on the hanger) might not relate to the larger arena of the stage. We call it "reading." Small patterns and some colors or details may be out of scale under the circumstances of distance and light. Some beautiful designer clothes, even authentic period pieces, are simply not emphatic enough to make a clear communication or statement to the audience. Be sure—especially if there is a direct script reference—that a costume carries out the playwright's intent. In *Hello, Dolly* Ernestina Money is described as wearing "buttercup yellow" and "baby pink shoes." That dress must be buttercup yellow. Anything less or lighter in hue won't read.

Remember that musicals are already a little larger than life. Every year fame and fortune are made by designers of musicals who win Tony awards. Professionals recognize the intelligence and talent of designers. They applaud all those who are so skillful and imaginative at making that special quality of the musical live so delightfully. Even old standards—such as Gilbert and Sullivan's *The Mikado*—can get a new look and spirit, even by adapting traditional Kabuki designs to modern treatments (figs. 18.2 and 18.3).

Professional Hints

A musical, with its large cast and varied abilities functioning as singers, dancers, and principals, can sometimes become a large, indistinguishable mass on stage. Consequently, without extensive and subtle lighting effects, action and focus are lost in a sea of bodies. Forget for a moment whether you will rent or borrow costumes and think of ways to "dress" your production. A few well-practiced techniques can help. If your show is *Oklahoma!* or *Bye Bye, Birdie,* use a common approach and dress the chorus in lighter colors and plainer clothes than the leads. One- or two-color chorus dresses contrast with the polka dot or striped costumes of the principals. The reverse also works, however. Have contrast work with you, not against you!

A standard rule in costuming is to factor in the "age" of your characters. They may all be teenagers in real life, but on stage we separate the older from the younger by color. General usage says that darker, somber, and muted colors suggest older personalities, where brighter, lighter colors are for the young. If you have an elderly man character who tries to be young and foolish, dress him in bright colors to emphasize his out-of-place behavior.

Color-coding families is another method used in professional design. Everyone in Romeo's family may be in varied shades and values of blue, while Juliet's family is dressed in tones and hues of red. Not only does it make it easier to follow a complex plot, it provides the designer with an aesthetic approach to designing. The idea of dressing a character so to recognize station and status goes back to the Greeks and Romans. Stop for a moment to think about this concept: most liturgical garments are color-coordinated with seasons and event. There's theatre everywhere!

In *My Fair Lady* and *The Sound of Music,* servants are dressed in black so that they will be unobtrusive. In Japanese drama, black is still considered "invisible." Noted costume teacher Raymond Sovey advised that servants always be dressed in fashions ten years behind the time period of the play to suggest that their clothes were hand-me-downs. The major lesson is that thinking about, rather than just choosing, clothes makes for success.

In one high school, owing to budgetary problems, students were told to supply their own costumes. Fortunately, the drama teacher in charge coordinated a motley array of clothing, suggesting a few exchanges and contributions. He worked with rented costumes, borrowed costumes, and homemade costumes effectively. It wasn't perfect, nor recommended, but it worked because of the teacher's skill and dedication.

On the other hand, a very well-intentioned costume committee of parents and friends helped an overwhelmed director with *Hello, Dolly.* They reasoned that since Dolly Levi was a widow in a very proper period of time, she should be dressed in mourning black. The costumes contradicted Dolly's personality and her pursuit of life, liberty, and Horace Vandergelder.

Just as blocking motivation helps to explain a character's feeling and behavior, so costuming defines and delineates who and what a character is. Whether you rent your costumes or pull them from a wardrobe collection, do it thoughtfully.

Makeup

Given the wash-out effect that stage lighting has on the human face, some reinforcement of features is necessary. We don't mean the kind of black-lined exaggeration sometimes used to try to make old age, but some evenly applied, subtly accented color that accents your actors. Remember, very bright light tends to make us look pale and wan and may flatten the shape of the head into a moon-face. Even dimmer light tends to make unpleasant hollows and makes it difficult to see an actor's expressions. A little makeup is not a dangerous thing.

Some performers feel that makeup prevents them from being natural or "themselves." Of course, they are not themselves; they are characters from a different place. A simple, unexaggerated foundation color, even from a cosmetic counter—a little darker or tan for men and a bit more bright or pink for women—can help offset the lighting effects.

Makeup companies offer instruction books and will even come to your school and do workshops. Consequently, we are limiting our discussion to general, but vital, tips. Makeup is an art akin to portrait painting, and many makeup artists have found careers in theatres.

Train your actors to do their own makeup and encourage them to practice many times. In the professional theatre, actors must be able to apply their own basic makeup. Good college theatre departments teach courses in the art.

A few cautions are in order:

- Never share makeup. Individual kits are available from reputable companies (see the bibliography).

- Makeup can spoil. It can go bad from time or harmful bacteria. Don't keep it for more than a year in normal temperatures.

- Avoid all exaggeration such as hard, dark lines for "wrinkles." All creases in nature flow like cloud effects.

- Men and boys don't normally need lipstick. Sometimes a darker foundation color is enough.

- Blend your makeup into your hairline.

- In makeup, "the *eyes* have it." They especially need accent, but not the old red dot used in ballet style.

- Makeup rubs off when you hug your admirers backstage.

Chapter 19
Lighting the Show

"Theatre" means "a seeing place," from the Greek *theatron*. The "seeing" is made possible in most dramatic productions by the lighting of the show. Professional lighting designers often feel that they make the show possible. They are not necessarily wrong. Ineffective lighting or lighting that is unsuitable for a production's intention can be a great distraction and even a destroyer of all the other artistic goals.

Lighting, one of the most specific of the design arts in theatre, is the most elusive. Lighting alone allows us to see the more absolute elements of sets and costumes. Yet it remains an abstract, because it isn't there until we see it. The fabric of the costume and the paint on the set remain under any condition. Thus, because of the inner visualness needed, lighting takes a special kind of sensitivity and understanding. Gifted lighting designers are a rare commodity.

Lighting is also the youngest of the theatre arts. Very early experiments were made with bottles, candles, and sconces during the Italian Renaissance. Being able to manage light through the dimming processes and color methods we use today only has been possible since Edison created the incandescent lamp in 1879. Nonetheless, lighting can affect changes in all the other aspects of sets, costumes, and actors. Hardly anything affects our psychological responses to seeing meaning in theatre as much as lighting does.

Development and invention in lighting control are changing so rapidly that any text written this year will suffer from omissions next year. Nonetheless, a good number of excellent texts on stage lighting are available (see the selected reading list) and are well worth investigating.

Incredible advancement in structural features of once basic instruments makes real expertise necessary. There are some very fundamental facts of lighting that will not change, however, especially in terms of color and direction. We will offer information that can be helpful and effective in dealing with lighting concepts when there is limited equipment and control. It is hard to imagine school or community theatres possessing the state of the art of Broadway or Las Vegas productions. Even so, learn all that you can about what is happening in the contemporary theatre industry. This knowledge stimulates ideas and gives opportunities for freshness and artistic challenges.

Characteristics of Light

Few directors realize that as an incandescent lamp is dimmed or faded in intensity, the light goes strongly yellow or amber in color. If one has chosen subtle lavenders, violets, and mauves for costumes, they are apt to go grey as the lights dim. The effect, in ballet and modern dance, can be disastrous. A beautiful scene suddenly leaves us feeling morose. Don't scream at the lighting designer—blame the laws of physics. Can one avoid traps such as this? The answer is "Yes!"

Lighting Instruments

Learn something about the basic instruments in lighting design and what they can do for you. Find out what positions are most useful for these instruments and what is apt to occur with most standard school or small theatre equipment. It is safe to say that every school stage in the United States has strip lights in standard use. These are long rows of lights contained in metal troughs and colored with glass rondels in the usual colors of red, green or yellow, and blue. Occasionally, every third or fourth light is left white. These strips, which may also be referred to as borders, are common in auditoriums, providing general illumination to every part of the stage. Non-focusable, they are indiscriminate, except for the rondel color.

If your school or community theatre has in-house lights with permanent wiring, these are likely Fresnels (pronounced "fren-nell") and Lekos, two industry standards now made in a variety of types with some exceptional capabilities.

The Fresnel is named after Augustin Jean Fresnel (1788–1827). Even though Fresnel had died by the time Edison built the incandescent lamp, the lens used in the Fresnel is a type invented by Fresnel for lighthouse beacons. The Leko, named for its creators Levy and Cook, is often referred to in catalogues as a Klieglight, or an ERS (ellipsoidal reflector spotlight). These two instruments exist in many makes and varieties and have two very different characteristics, and so each has a different function on the stage.

The primary usefulness of a Fresnel is in providing a soft, enveloping area light. Its beam may be shaped mechanically to be round or oval. Because it tends to be a spreading light with soft, diffused edges, it is most commonly used overhead and not from a great distance. The Fresnel is excellent for blending tones and colors together and is very kind to actors. The light is not harsh and seems to surround the object or persons on which it falls. The term "special" is applied to a light used to delineate a sofa, chair, or playing area, with the source usually a Fresnel. The color of a Fresnel light is altered by inserting a gel frame with choice of color in front of the lens. A small focus area (called spot) or a large focus area (called flood) is easily achieved by sliding or moving the lamp inside the housing (fig. 19.1).

The Leko, or ERS, is the odd-shaped instrument one usually sees in profusion on the audience side of the proscenium or attached to the front of the balcony in any professional production (fig. 19.2). This instrument has a very powerful beam of light that can be focused to have very sharp edges. If one wished to light *only* the doorway at the top of the stairs of Harmonia Gardens in *Hello, Dolly,* a Leko would be used. It is also the best device for lighting overlapping areas across the front of the stage for an even tone or wash.

Techniques

It is not the purpose of this book to cover lighting design in great detail (which is already covered in many excellent texts), so we will point out only a few pertinent but valuable facts that may enhance your production.

Basically speaking, light can only come from four directions on stage:

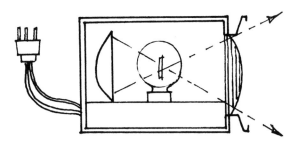

Fig. 19.1. The Fresnel instrument showing area spread of light.

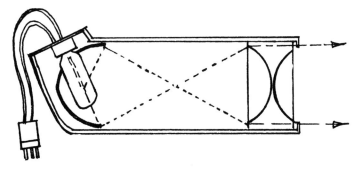

Fig. 19.2. The Leko instrument, or ERS, showing focused beam of light.

- Front

- Side

- Overhead

- Back

Frontlighting is strictly illumination most of the time. It helps us see and "feel" a sensation through intensity and color. In German, *einfuhling* ("in-feeling") implies that the inner response one gets from outward stimuli is a single sensation. Good front-lighting can offer this quality.

Sidelighting has become the industry standard for modern dance and ballet. Some dance lighting designers adamantly refuse to use anything *except* sidelight for dance. Designers place ERS lights very low on offstage booms to illuminate steps and foot actions. Because of their placement these lamps are known to dancers and stage hands as "shinbusters."

Overhead lighting, especially from a "bridge" position or first electric pipe immediately behind the teaser, will not only cover various areas, but may be thought of as the main dramatic light. Falling on the heads and shoulders of actors, usually from Fresnels, overhead light is best for creating a dramatic effect. This character of light seems particularly dramatic when the actor is lit from an angle (instead of straight down). Overhead light combined with front light adds considerable dimension to the actors' performances.

The most neglected lighting concept in amateur productions is **backlight.** More often than not, this is due to a lack of equipment, and/or circuits or control, rather than neglect. This is unfortunate, because backlighting is similar to the third dimension of a piece of sculpture. Striking the actor from behind, it indeed sculpts the actor's head and upper body. It sets off actors against the often complicated scenery. Technically, backlighting occurs from an overhead position, but the distinction between the two is valid.

Characteristics of Color

A good lighting designer will choose a backlight color that creates an aura, or glow, around the body without being obvious or distracting. Sometimes a contrasting backlight tone is necessary for a musical's dance sequences. Without some backlight, your staging seems "flattened out."

It is impossible to cover here everything one ought to be aware of concerning lighting's color. Two points must be stressed, however:

1. Light has primary and secondary color characteristics, just as paint does. These characteristics are not the same in light as in paint.

2. Light color may be adjusted or altered by the use of color filters (gels).

Wavelengths of light can be broken down into three primary colors, namely *red, green,* and *blue*. The overlapping of these colors produces the secondary colors in light as follows:

- Red and green produce amber, a yellowish light.

- Red and blue produce magenta, a lavender light.

- Blue and green produce cyan, a turquoise light.

Mixing all three primary colors maintained at the same intensity tends to produce white light. Mixing any two secondary colors also tends to create a whitish light. When a different color in light is made by the use of two or more color filters, it is called additive mixing. This must usually be accomplished with two (or more) sources of light. If two or more color filters are placed in front of one light source, the process is called subtractive mixing.

A director may prefer to leave the technical elements to the respective designers. Often, though, you may be perceiving an odd "look" about the scenery and costumes that is the result of light and color. At such a time, being able to deduce what might have happened is helpful. Let us suppose, for instance, that you have painted a stage set for Desiree's bedroom in *A Little Night Music* a charming feminine lavender, but the only lighting your limited system can provide is the amber used for previous outdoor scenes. The result is probably a gray, lifeless scene.

While the primary colors of light are somewhat different from the primary colors of paint (red, yellow, blue), the interaction between the two mediums is approximately the same. In both mediums we have primary and secondary colors, and the mixing of these will tend to neutralize one color or the other. Quite simply, red light on a green set will make it look blackened. Green light on a pink costume will make it gray, or even brown, in appearance. How can this be avoided? Broadway musical productions use computer technology and Vari-Lites, color scrollers, Pani projectors, and Cyberlights, etc., to create almost any effect. Even though your theatre probably does not have access to such equipment, learn all that you can about what is happening in the theatre industry to stimulate ideas.

Gels

Lighting designers have color filters, also called generically "gels." Gels may be used in special frames on lighting instruments to create any compatible, motivated, and interpretive effect desired. But you must be willing to learn, experiment, and find out what happens with your choices of paint, fabrics, and makeup. With a selection of color filters of many types available, one may choose from two or three hundred possibilities. Color changers and dozens of automatic devices now make the technology of lighting and scenic design limited only by our own imaginations.

The Cue Sheet

A cue sheet indicates directly where and when each major or minor lighting effect takes place. Just as your prompt book should include all your cues, warnings for scene changes, curtains, exits, and entrances, so should it note all lighting effects. The lighting designer will create a light plot to designate the placement and direction of lighting instruments. The designer will also carefully notate the cue sheet (fig. 19.3). Even Tony award-winning lighting designers generally develop a "magic" sheet that allows an instant recognition of where a light is supposed to be and permits instant changes if there is a lamp failure or a mistake.

| | | | PRESETS | |
Scene	Page	Action	out of	into
Act I		House open: house lites/ 7	works	01 & 02
	2	House to half, then out	OVERTURE	
	14	Curtain warmers: music cue	01	
	14	Add "fans" to sky	02	03
	15	Silhouette: slow fade up	03	04
ff	21	Nanki Poo enters	04	05
	31	Pish Tush enters	05	11
ff	32	Music: Pish Tush song	11	12
	41	Restore full	12	13
	42	Pooh Bah on gesture	13	14
	47	(Set change) Bamboo in Fans out	14	15
	48	Men's song	15	21
	49	Ko Ko's entrance UL	21	22
	55	Ko Ko speech on BRIDGE	22	23
ff	56	Ko Ko song (Little list)	23	24
	62	Restore full	24	25
	63	Men's chorus	25	31
	69	Women: THREE LITTLE MAIDS	31	32
	76	Restore	32	33
	77	"So Please you,Sir"	33	34
	87	Restore	34	35
	88	Duet	35	41
	92	Restore	41	42
		page <u>one of four</u>		
		cue sheets and design by Thomas J. Blalock		

Fig. 19.3. Lighting designer's cue sheet (for *The Mikado*).

Part III
PERFORMANCE

Chapter 20
Small Things Count

"We've got magic to do" is a lyric of the song that begins the musical *Pippin*. Theatre, all of it, is magic. Magicians who reveal the secrets of their craft before performance have no magic to weave. Directors should remember that their secrets ought to be hidden until the curtain opens or the play begins.

Too many nonprofessional productions seem oblivious to this fact. It seems a concerted effort is made to dispel the illusion of theatre as the audience is filling the seats. Actors and production personnel dash hither and yon, across the stage, through the curtains, on the stage setting. This is opposed to the very nature of theatre, on any level. Again, everything in theatre happens AFTER the curtain goes up.

People go to the theatre in the same frame of mind reserved for ceremony or celebration. Good theatre should be a magic experience, whether it is pure entertainment or Greek drama.

What Constitutes a Performance?

A performance's cast is confident, unharried, sufficiently rehearsed and instructed, and has stamina and talent. Your much-anticipated and worked-for presentation before an audience begins the day you cast your play. Every detail of the script and every decision regarding production must be thought of in relationship to its potential effect upon the audience. Don't solve problems quickly as a convenience or merely dismiss them during your preparation period. One often hears a director say, "We can fix it later." Later may never happen.

Run-throughs

In a more practical sense, however, your performance will start to take on a realistic shape when you arrive at run-throughs. Usually started a week or two before opening night, run-throughs are pretend performances. This is where a competent, experienced stage manager takes over. The cast and stage crew, under the direction of the stage manager, run the full show without interruptions. Should there be some disaster or miscue of great proportion, the director must step in to resolve it. The run-through should naturally involve an accompanist, music director, and (preferably) an orchestra conductor.

Although run-throughs do not usually include a full orchestra, it is important for timing, cues, and visual direction that the conductor "stand in" for complete ensemble. Be certain that the entire cast and crew are present during run-throughs. Their commitment is essential.

Notes

For the director and assistant, one of the key purposes of the run-through is to start polishing the production. Every detail that may not look as well as it could is recorded—or noted—by both of them. This is the source of the "notes," taken to improve the show, given to the cast by the director.

Notes may, for example, include

- Should Character A wait for an audience reaction, or laugh, before continuing dialogue with Character B?

- What speech wasn't clearly delivered, or what end of a line was lost in a hasty exit?

- Should the kiss be restaged so that we see the girl's face instead of the boy's?

- Is the ensemble reacting appropriately at the right time to the business on stage?

Giving the notes to the cast is critical; when to do it is a matter of personal preference and technique. We recommend going over notes immediately after the run-through rehearsal, if possible. At this point, things are still fresh and easy to adjust, alter, or change. Once technical and dress rehearsals begin, however, it is suggested that you reserve notes until the beginning of the next rehearsal.

Inasmuch as nonprofessional productions do not have the distinct advantage of previews or out-of-town tryouts, consider taking notes during the first two or three performances to see what has worked or been effective with an audience. Some directors prefer not to do this, feeling that the "job" is done by that time, but in school and community theatre teaching goes on all the time.

If set changes seem to present a problem, the solution is simply to call for a crew rehearsal under the direction of the stage manager. Directors need to have a lot of patience and understanding with the production crews. It is often forgotten that the actors have six or ten weeks to prepare, while technical crews may have only a night or two. They are usually expected to know what to do merely from watching. The technical production needs are often not satisfied that way.

A check of a typical rehearsal schedule shows that two weeks of run-throughs are indicated. Excessive? Not at all. Letting the cast run the play on its own helps them to feel the rhythm of a show and develop a pace consistent with its style. It also drives home the message of each individual responsibility.

Costume Parade

A "costume parade" is very helpful during the run-through period because it allows the coordination of lights, sets, and costumes. A costume parade is a rehearsal devoted entirely to seeing the actors (dressed for performance) walk through various scenes in order to check color effects and style or materials. Professionally it is a must. Community theatre may find it more advantageous to conduct a regular run-through rehearsal in costume so that suitability can be assessed. This allows the committee to see what's missing or what doesn't fit. Do this at least one week before dress rehearsal.

If you are staying with a realistic and typical schedule, by the time you are having run-throughs the sets are nearing completion, and piece by piece, they appear on stage. Actually spacing out your rehearsals with costumes, sets, and lights, in order to have them occur sequentially instead of all at once, is a device that gradually builds a performance mentality in your cast. Actors gain confidence and credibility as the pieces come together.

This is a particular time for caution, however. There is a moment in the rehearsal period that directors have come to know as the "slump" when everyone's energy level seems to fade. Why it happens is never clear, as it may happen at different times and for no apparent reason at all. It does appear to occur shortly after the cast becomes secure in knowing their lines and business. Is the anxiety level down? Is it overconfidence? Most likely not; the production just needs a new impetus, a new force to propel itself. The costume parade, cue-to-cue, and tech rehearsals usually help.

What should you do as the director? Be supportive. The cast needs to know that you believe in their abilities and that this is a natural occurrence. Never belittle a cast or crew simply to demonstrate your more "professional" experience. It will likely have the opposite effect on their assessment of you.

Cue-to-Cue

Assuming that your sets, costumes, and lighting are as complete as can be to enhance and support your production, it is time for a "cue-to-cue" rehearsal. This is a vital step. It is often overlooked in nonprofessional theatre, usually with dire results. A cue-to-cue rehearsal is conducted by the stage manager, beginning with the opening of the main curtain or the starting point of the show. If there are house lights to be dimmed or turned off, do so. Everything should be done as if the audience were present. Actors are instructed to speak the opening lines. The stage manager will then stop them and move ahead in the script to the first change of lighting, sets, props, or music, including sound effects that may be called for offstage. As each cue is rehearsed and the crews are instructed in what is supposed to happen, the cue is repeated and the crew business done in order to see that everyone knows precisely what his or her job is to be.

All actors, singers, and dancers should be present to be aware of the dangers of sets being moved and to time costume changes with music numbers. It is not necessary to deliver all dialogue or sing each song all the way through. Instruct performers to realize that they will be stopped in the midst of a song—no matter how pretty it is or delightfully it is being performed—to move to the next cue.

A cue-to-cue rehearsal can be bad or good.

> **Bad:** If the directors, or other designers, have not done their work well, a cue-to-cue may be exasperating, frustrating, and very long.
>
> **Good:** When a cue-to-cue accomplishes its goal, you end the rehearsal feeling confident about the technical production values.

Technical Rehearsal

A tech (technical) rehearsal generally follows the cue-to-cue rehearsal. Usually, it's the next practice, after school or in the evening. This rehearsal is as full as it can possibly be (with the possible exception of the orchestra players) and should be conducted, once again, as if it were a performance. This is the only opportunity the crews will have to perfect what they have learned at the cue-to-cue; however, its main purpose will be to see that no insurmountable technical problems occur. If there should be a serious mistake in a lighting cue—for instance, the midnight scene comes on in full daylight—the rehearsal should stop to fix the problem.

Then, at last, the days of dress rehearsals are upon you.

Dress Rehearsals

Dress rehearsals are exactly that. With full sets, costumes, makeup, lights, orchestra, and crews, dress rehearsals are to be done as if the audience were in place. Everyone must be alert to all cues and business. There can be no missed lines, words, or props.

The old adage that a bad dress rehearsal means a good performance is not generally true. The only positive impact a bad dress rehearsal might have is finally driving home the message that the cast, crew, and director have to work harder and be more alert to the possible pitfalls in performance.

The Stage Manager

The stage manager takes over as completely as possible at this point. In the professional theatre it is said that the stage manager takes charge "without qualification"—in other words, completely. The person most essential for successful performances is the stage manager.

Before rehearsals, the stage manager posts a sign-in sheet on the backstage callboard for each dress and performance call. Everyone, from crew to director, must sign in at least one hour before the scheduled rehearsal time. In professional theatre, Equity rules require actors to report at least one-half hour before curtain time.

Before the actual rehearsal begins, the stage manager will

1. Be the first to arrive to begin checks on all cast, crew, and technical requirements. (Special note: If the director gives notes before a performance, the stage manager should call the cast together, as requested, at an appropriate time and place. Other chores are sweeping the stage (if not assigned to the properties crew) and collecting and securing the cast's valuables.)

2. Check that all props, sets, and "running" equipment are in place.

3. Clear the stage for a light instrument check, ensuring that all instruments are working and that dimming is operating.

4. Check intercoms and headsets with all areas.

5. Review curtain procedures with house manager at least one half hour before curtain.

6. Give cast and crew the "half-hour" call. All actors and crew normally answer the stage manager's call with a "Thank you!" indicating they have heard the warning.

7. Give cast and crew a "fifteen-minute" call.

8. Check with house manager and box office for smooth procedure.

9. Give cast and crew a "three-minute" call. A "three-minute" call tells all actors and crew to go immediately to places for the start of the show, insuring that everything is in place. If there is an unforeseen emergency (late audience due to storms, for example), a "five-minute hold" call is made. No actors or crew should leave the set.

10. On signal from the house manager that all is well, or that the "house is in," the stage manager begins the show.

In the professional theatre the stage manager's post is usually a position backstage where everything can be seen and supervised. All cues are called for from this position. Many theatres, such as the Metropolitan Opera House, have elaborate closed circuit video arrangements with which the stage manager can instantly spot scene change operation and crew locations. Through headset intercoms, the stage manager is responsible for giving the curtain cues and all subsequent cues for lighting effects, sound warnings, and changes of scene.

Opening Cues

An example of the stage manager's cues after the house manager informs that "the house is in" follows.

Stage Manager's Cue	Operators on Headsets Reply
(1) Thank you. House to half, please.	(1) House to half.
(2) One minute to curtain.	(2) One minute to curtain.
(3) Curtain warmers in please, house out.	(3) Curtain warmers up.
(4) Ready curtain.	(4) Ready.
(5) Go curtain.	(5) Curtain go.
(6) Cue one.	(6) Cue up.

If this seems tedious, time-consuming, or even overly efficient, remember that these practices are based on professional operation, where every element is carefully reiterated for each performance so that a stage manager can give absolute, accurate artistry to a long-running production. Curtain should go up at the announced time. It is a compliment and a show of respect for those who have arrived on time. The stage manager's work "before the scenes" can insure that you start your production when promised. If he or she has done the job, you will never hold a curtain because you aren't ready. The continued success of the show and a healthy box office return depend on such efficiency.

Little Oversights—Big Trouble

There are times when even an excellent performance by a talented cast and a skillful director can be marred by little errors we haven't had time to correct. Some things seem to be such "common sense" that we even forget them until it's too late. A favorite student used to proclaim, "The trouble with 'common' sense is . . . it ain't!"

Actors should never, never appear in the lobby or audience areas in costume and makeup. Keep the magic on the stage. Greet your friends in your own clothes or after the performance.

A small thing can destroy a scene or even an entire production. It can happen when an actor laughs at his own dialogue or business. For the sake of a good performance, and certainly to accomplish your best theatrical goals, train your actors to "stay in character!"

Many a school production has been sabotaged by the teacher who agrees to be in the "senior class musical" but grins throughout the performance or nods approval to the "kids" sharing the stage.

Actors need to learn to listen to what is being spoken, to respond in some appropriate and spontaneous way, and to pick up cues. An actor may listen intently to a previous line but then have a delayed reaction to it. It may only be three seconds, but it seems an eternity. In real life, we react and respond as soon as the other person stops talking.

Here's a list of additional troublesome little details no one thought to mention:

- Warn actors, crew, and stagehands not to brush against or push aside the stage curtains when entering or exiting. The necessary "legs" or wings should be treated as invisible or nonexistent. Brushing or pushing them reminds us of the unreality of being on stage.

- Crew, or stage hands, should always be dressed in black or dark colors (including socks). They, too, are invisible. T-shirts with messages will not fit in with your production.

- Check your programs for spelling errors. Schools and colleges ought to be particularly careful.

- Make sure the cast members onstage aren't "peeking" through the curtain or surreptitiously waving to family and friends.

- Forbid the use of cameras and recording devices. Flashbulbs may cause an actor to lose his train of thought, or worse, create a distraction that makes a dancer fall and be injured.

- There seems to be a growing trend among audiences to behave as if they were at home watching TV and get up and go out for a smoke any old time. Warn your actors.

- Be careful of orchestral pauses. To keep that "seamless flow" watch for the second or two interval it takes for a singer to wait for a downbeat. A long music intro can threaten the mood and meaning of a song.

- Train your cast to watch the conductor without being obvious. Train the eye and ear to work together.

- Large choruses tend to wait for "someone else" to start the action-reaction. They must look attentive and alive at all times. Make the play look as if it happens for the first time every time. That's professional!

- Your cast's reactions, especially those conveying a sense of honest enjoyment, are contagious. Smiles, in the proper places, project a sincere feeling of fun. A misplaced smirk or sneer at moments of sadness can be really tragic. The "fun" of Gilbert and Sullivan, for instance, is making the audience believe the players "believe" all the bizarre and preposterous twists of plot and character. Only in Gilbert and Sullivan, and maybe *Little Mary Sunshine,* are we permitted to guffaw at adversity.

Superstitions

The theatre world is full of superstitions about performing, acting, and general backstage deportment. Many practices may be "local" in origin, harking back in time to an event that became area drama lore.

One universal "never do" is to whistle backstage. It's supposed to be bad luck. This superstition has potential origins in nineteenth-century English theatre, when out-of-work sailors were stagehands and whistling signals were used to communicate. An inadvertent whistle at the wrong moment might have brought scenery crashing down off cue!

It's also considered bad luck to wish an actor "good luck." The backward logic of superstition, therefore, demands offering bad luck if an actor is to have good luck. Thus, the favorite expression of good will in theatre is "Break a leg!"

Curtain Calls

We eagerly await those moments ending the evening when we relish the applause, cheers, and bravos we hope we deserve. Directors and theatre practitioners differ somewhat regarding curtain calls. A sampling:

- Some directors will not practice curtain calls at all, considering them bad luck. Other directors explain in detail what they want but will not run through the procedure. One explanation: It isn't part of the play.

- Another director rehearses curtain calls several days ahead in order to make them "look like part of the play."

- Most directors practice curtain calls after the final dress rehearsal, unless they are having preview performances; then, they might be rehearsed after the first preview.

- Some directors do not have curtain calls at all. Their explanation is that they "may detract from the play's impact" or are not appropriate to a serious dramatic piece, such as *Man of La Mancha*.

- Other directors insist on group or ensemble curtain calls, because "we are a company" and are "all in this together."

Most of us *want* to show our appreciation for the accomplishment of the performers and the quality of the production. Audiences feel welcome and involved when honored with a thoughtful and well-crafted curtain call. It may make them feel inclined to come back again to see your group.

Make your call spirited, energetic, and "professional." To be spirited, it should move along quickly, each actor or pair of actors quickly following previous bows. Energetic actors will stride forward to accept applause confidently and graciously. Many an amateur spoils a creditable performance with a kind of desultory, grim-faced bow, partly from embarrassment and partly from not knowing "how" to bow. If necessary, teach your actor to walk quickly and confidently to center stage, stop feet together, and bend at the waist with arms at his sides. The splayed arm bow, done while still walking through center stage, is awkward and uncomfortable. Then, he will move immediately to an assigned position in the group. Remind him that the bow is for the actor, not necessarily for the character. Only on the rarest of occasions does one see a professional do a "character turn" while accepting curtain call applause.

Your curtain call should be well-rehearsed—and without special speeches and ceremonies—effectively bringing your "magic" theatre experience to a close. If it is your school's tradition to hand out awards and gifts, do so when all bows are complete: recall the cast and crew or re-open the curtain. Those interested surely will stay.

Your leading actor should be the one to acknowledge the orchestra and conductor in the curtain call applause, stepping forward to indicate these very essential performers.

Chapter 21
Getting the Word Out

Early is the word for publicity.

We are often deeply involved in getting a production up "on the boards" when questions arise about publicity. How do we make the public aware of what we are doing, and how much can we spend? Consider carefully some of your options in public media or print. Plan for them or pay for them, as the case may be, but do it, and above all, do it early.

Possible Methods

Experienced community groups probably have practiced methods in place already. School groups also know what their audience potential is, according to the size of the student body and typical parent support for other events, and have discovered corresponding means of advertising their shows. Indeed, in many schools the "spring musical" is the event of the year, and your problem may not be attracting an audience, but what to do in case of a standing room only crowd. This, by the way, is a situation to be researched through your building inspector or local fire department. You need to know if standees are allowed, and, if so, what is the maximum number.

We have not found any standard operating procedure that will be applicable to all groups or institutions. Why? Many schools that are regional in nature don't have immediate access to billboard advertising, for one thing; many local newspapers have policies that may actually discourage numerous weekly articles and pictures. Posters, which we will speak about, are not welcome in most chain stores or malls.

So what *can* you do? Take stock of all the possibilities, eliminate some, if necessary, and compensate through other venues:

- Commercial billboards are an excellent means of reaching a wide audience. Some companies are very interested in offering rates as public service announcements. Lead time for preparation is important, so check early.

- Posters are an inexpensive means of advertising. Have a design contest, which in itself creates some publicity. Posters must be competitive, however, because many groups use this medium. Posters have a short life of ten days to two weeks. Use them as an initial saturation device and make sure they are readable from a distance.

- Clever flyers or handbills playing off the show's title may be (with permission) left in churches, libraries, and schools, or may be mailed to a list of previous ticket buyers.

- Attractive placemats are not inexpensive, but they can reach many people, including tourists, if your local restaurants are cooperative. A small cardboard "tent," however, is a very effective means of advertising if local diners, restaurants, or eateries will use them. Be courteous and replace them every five to ten days.

- Processors can easily print out a postcard that may be used as a handout whenever someone asks about your show or for mailings.

- Are there empty store windows in your town? An attractive display window with costumed mannequins, banners, and ticket information can work well for you, and for the store owner.

- Find out well ahead of time if your newspaper has any particular policy regarding press releases. You may feel that it's news when the school principal will appear as Horace Vandergelder, but they may not. In order to be fair to all organizations that present public performances, they may limit your news articles and number of pictures. Lead articles or big cast announcements are generally not run more than ten days ahead of performances. Remember, if you want pictures, set aside time and costumes for effective promotional uses. Experience has proven that every time a clear ad appears in the pages of a newspaper or "pennysaver," the reservation phone-line gets busy.

- Display ads are the most effective media at your disposal.

- In a small newspaper, perhaps even a weekly, a personal ad offers a charming and clever way to advertise.

- T-shirts and buttons featuring the name of the show are easily manufactured, usually locally (through a print shop), and make great cast and crew souvenirs.

- If you have two or three dress/tech rehearsals, you may invite special senior citizen groups or school classes, and their enthusiasm can sell lots of tickets.

- Newspaper reviews sell many tickets if your production is playing a "run." If you are giving only two or three performances, the review may not be published in time to help you. Lately, many local papers have refused to "write up" student and community theatre productions for fear of hurting feelings or losing customers. Such policies may be "bad" or "good" depending on the quality of your news reviewers.

- Without a doubt, when the audience loves your production, and the word gets around that you are "almost professional," your ticket sales will soar. Word-of-mouth publicity is the best there is! Many a Broadway show has been panned by critics but saved by the audiences who found something the reviewers missed.

- Can you afford television? If you envision a filmed video clip of your show in progress or a sophisticated graphic display, probably not. There are, however, some public service announcements and some community bulletin board notices available if you have a local cable network. Be reminded, once again, that there are restrictive deadlines, often as much as a month in advance, for these notices. Lots of local networks feature weekend programs of cultural attractions and may even provide a "talk show" format for your group. Legally, you must once again be careful of copyright laws covering the electronic use of songs, scenes, or episodes of your musical.

- Radio stations are a very viable and important means of reaching lots of people. In our area the local radio has done more to help organizations through interviews, public service announcements, and thirty-second ads than any other media. Radio music programs like to offer free tickets to call-in listeners, and this is a clever way to reach new audiences.

Publicity, like budgets, varies from one community to another, especially from a metropolitan area to a rural one. In both instances we advise that you begin early with a very realistic plan or campaign with known expectations of your efforts. Can you get sufficient coverage in your newspaper or through your school? If not, plan another way to inform the public of your production.

Even if you do not have an accomplished graphic artist or designer in your organization, many play booking agencies offer poster and publicity packages for a moderate price.

The Box Office

Rapport with your audience begins the moment they try to contact you for tickets. Be sure you have an efficient but polite procedure for dealing with both personal and telephone orders. The ticket seller may be harried and hurried, but must remain cool at all times.

Sometimes loyal audience members, or playgoers, want to have a "chat" with the seller about other productions they have seen, and as a consequence information about dates, prices, and number of seats required may be neglected.

Plan a prerehearsed technique for giving information over the phone, and be sure it is consistent. What time is curtain? When should tickets be picked up? Do you accept credit cards? Are all the seats "good"? Will I miss much if I'm ten minutes late? Be sure to mention that you have a latecomers policy (that should be reasonable but efficient).

Often a production simply takes off and becomes a word-of-mouth hit, and ticket requests far exceed expectations. Sometimes this creates a pileup at the box office, with curtain time dangerously close. Have extra help on hand; divide reservations into alphabetical groups for quick search; separate out season ticket holders; and be careful about money. Don't leave an evening's receipts unattended or a ticket seller all alone after the curtain is up.

Complimentary tickets are much appreciated by people who have loaned props or costumes or simply been helpful. "Annie Oakleys," or free tickets, are given to businesses that may have provided pizzas for your cast and crew during rehearsals or donated financial support to your school production.

To avoid confusion, professional theatres all use tickets coordinated with seat numbers or a seating plan. As one enters a theatre from the back of the house, or the lobby, the even numbered seats, such as A 2, 4, 6, 8, and so on, are to your right, and the odd numbers, such as C 1, 3, 5, 7, 9, are on the left. If there is a center section, seats are usually numbered in the hundred series, for example, A 101, 102, 103, from right to left. In spite of this general practice, newcomers often wonder if they will sit together. It pays to have a sense of humor if you are a theatre usher. Most school auditoriums offer seating by general admission, because it is certainly easier to keep track of a total number of seats sold rather than individual reservations.

The common practice in professional theatres is to seat latecomers at the first scene change or even after an act. It is especially hard for a performer to sing a song while latecomers troop up and down the aisle.

When people are treated politely, made to feel welcome, and even thanked for coming after the show is over, they will be back again and again. It is part of the "audience development" technique. It works.

Chapter 22
Mounting the Show

In school and community productions you must be prepared for the unexpected more often than you might wish. Some schools have very strict attitudes about using the auditorium. Rules made for the protection of the facility are necessary, even when they place obstacles in the path of a theatrical endeavor. Respect those rules by working within them, and two things happen: first, you avoid alienating custodial staff and administrators; second, accepting unusual restrictions may increase your imaginative possibilities.

Do's and Don'ts

If putting nails or screws in the highly polished stage floor is forbidden, using "book" flats (see chapter 17) or wagons that roll is really a better way of envisioning your set.

We have had much experience with what should be reputable companies storming into a rented or loaned facility only to disparage it and disregard rules. Our feeling is that real artists, even Shakespearean actors, should express their talent with intelligence, not arrogance. Try to remember that respect for others is respect for yourself—as either an artist or a person.

Community theatre groups that do not have their own stages and must rent encounter restrictions on time and, sometimes, equipment. Find out well ahead of time what you can or cannot do! All of these situations lead back to the need for planning and preparation months ahead.

Having assisted numerous school and community theatre productions, we find remarkable unanimity on several points:

- Don't get paint on the floor (use dropcloths).

- Don't put nails or screws in the floor.

- Don't scratch the floor. (If it's been waxed, dancers beware!)

- Don't interfere with classes, assemblies, or speakers.

- Don't make noise during the day.

- Don't get paint on the drapes.

- Make sure everything is movable.

While any or all of these requests may be inconvenient, none of them is unreasonable. All the school personnel we have dealt with have been tremendously cooperative with struggling teacher-directors, but at the same time they worry a great deal.

The physical difficulties you may encounter in the typical school or community auditorium are more serious. Usually you will find

- No flyspace, or nothing much over ten to fifteen feet of height

- No wing space to hide scenery or cast members

- A very wide proscenium built for assemblies

You can handle all of these exigencies. A good book on scenic art (see the bibliography) will tell you how to double-hang backdrops or use a rigging method that will fold a drop as a roman shade gathers. Staircases that must look as if they actually go upstairs can be effectively suggested by a "landing" and hidden upstairs. Wing space may be created by flats constructed to be scenery or to blend with your set design as "legs." Cut down extreme width by designing a decorative proscenium of your own on either side of the stage. See figure 22.1 of *Oliver* from Mt. Greylock Regional High School for an example of scenic proscenium flats. Remember that every difficulty can be overcome with imagination and effort.

Fig. 22.1. Model with scenic proscenium flats, *Oliver,* Mt. Greylock Regional High School.

Safety

As the director—the person in charge—keep a "safety" sign blinking in your thoughts. Theatre is a physical thing. People, properties, and scenery are constantly moving. That means action, and action has the undercurrent of danger. Be exactly aware of everything that is going on in the theatre. Wishing someone to "break a leg" may be superstition to avoid trouble, but trouble is a grim reality when it actually happens. So take caution.

Be sure to try all of your physical tricks or maneuvers yourself to insure safety. A single case of inadvertent injury dampens the spirit of excitement for your whole production. Moreover, it may harm an overeager actor and bring about lawsuits for which you are liable. Note that all professional productions, especially Shakespearean, now have "fight coaches" or notices of "swordfights staged by. . . . " Seek help from your physical education teachers or karate experts in ways to fool the eye in stage battles. The wise thing to do is always to stop, think, and work out difficulties in a calmer moment.

Most modern theatres have a provision for a "ghost light," or spirit light, to be lit whenever the theatre is dark and unoccupied. It supposedly keeps the ghosts of earlier actors out, but more importantly, provides illumination for passing through what could be a very dark stage without walking off the edge and crashing into the orchestra pit. This light is a vital safety feature.

Smoking and eating backstage are generally avoided or not permitted. Eating makes conditions unsanitary or forces someone to be the "maid" who cleans up. Smoking is a fire and health hazard. Smoke interferes with the lighting effects and is hard on the singers' throats. One of the most important safety lessons to be learned by actors is how to be considerate of others. Our experience has shown that the most considerate actor is usually the one who is the biggest, truest "star."

Strike!

Notice the last word to close out the schedule is "strike." In theatre it is used for the dismantling and removal of the show's set, usually at the end of a production. Everything is included: flats, levels, stair units, furniture, and props. The term can also mean to remove a prop or article from the stage. The director, or stage manager, may say to a stage hand, "Strike that bench."

Hopefully the scene designer has considered this final task during his design process. Scenic units are

- Those that are saved and stored for possible future use

- Those that are consigned to oblivion in the dumpster

- Those, such as furniture and props, that have been borrowed and must be returned

The cost of the show's strike must be included in the budget, even on Broadway. There is a wonderful scene in Moss Hart's *Light Up the Sky* when a novice playwright asks what happens to all the scenery if the show is a flop. The leading lady's jaded mother replies, "Pray for a windy day on the dump." It neatly conveys the idea that the faster the sets can be disposed of, the less expensive they will be.

Colleges often have a policy of holding the strike immediately after the final performance. Cast members are required to participate. This is usually necessary to accomodate scheduling of the theatre. High schools may approach the job more leisurely, scheduling the dismantling and storage on weekends or after school. Some hold the strike the Sunday after the last Saturday night performance. Oddly, perhaps, this has a definite, positive psychological effect. The spirit of the cast and crew is still high, and few tears are shed. Actors often take home pieces of the set.

This event might also be an excellent time to get parents involved, lending support to your performing arts goals and guidance as well. Wahconah Regional High School, Dalton, Massachusetts, has a policy of bringing in fathers, mothers, brothers, sisters, and other relatives to help build sets, as well as take them down. Some also get involved in costuming, sewing, and prop making. The result has been an entire community solidly behind the drama program, which is mainly extracurricular, and a guaranteed full house at performances.

The strike, well supervised and planned for, can be a very good lesson in safety, discipline, and planning, particularly for the student who later becomes a teacher-director. Keep in mind it is part of the total theatre experience. It needn't be drudgery; make it rewarding!

Appendix

"Musicals! The Perfect Medicine!"

by Christopher Rawson

If you want to feel better about the world today, the perfect medicine is the high school musical in your own town or neighborhood.

It's no accident that the musical traditionally comes in March or April, when the sap is starting to run and the buds starting to open. Youthful energy is the heart of this goofy, exhausting rite of spring.

"The play's the thing," we like to say, but that's only partly true of this annual burst of creative enthusiasm. The audience is also very much the thing, the gaggle of proud families and fellow students, from giggling admirers to cool ironists.

Many drama critics around the country won't go to high school musicals, let alone write about them. They can't know what they're missing. I could get to only five this year, but each one proved a distinctive pleasure . . . the kids themselves, performers, musicians, crew and friends—slick, knobby, jerky, svelte, frenetic, gangly, intense and cool, sometimes simultaneously, sometimes by turns. What a rich feast of individual achievement and promise.

Selected Reading List

Directing

Cohen, Robert, and John, Harrop. *Creative Play Direction*. Englewood Cliffs, N.J.: Prentice-Hall, Inc., 1974.

Engel, Lehman. *The American Musical Theatre: A Consideration*. New York: A CBS Legacy Collection Book, Distr. by MacMillan Co., 1967.

————. *The Complete Guidebook for Producing a Musical in Your Theater*. New York: Schirmer Books/Division of MacMillan Publishing Co., 1983.

Filichia, Peter. *Let's Put on a Musical!* New York: Avon Books, 1993.

Grote, David. *Staging the Musical: Planning, Rehearsing, and Marketing the Amateur Production*. Englewood Cliffs, N.J.: A Spectrum Book, Prentice-Hall, Inc., 1986.

Opelt, James R. *Organizing and Managing the High School Theatre Program*. Needham Heights, Mass.: Allyn and Bacon, Division of Simon and Schuster, 1991.

Smith, Milton. *Play Production*. New York: D. Appleton-Century Company, Appleton-Century-Crofts, 1962.

Stern, Lawrence. *Stage Management*. 5th ed. Needham, Mass.: Allyn and Bacon, A Simon and Schuster Company, 1995.

Vaughn, Stuart. *Directing Plays: A Working Professional's Method*. White Plains, N.Y.: Longman Publishing Group, 1993.

Acting

Albright, Hardie. *The Creative Process*. Encino, Calif.: Dickenson Publishing Co., 1974.

Benedetti, Robert L. *The Actor at Work*. Englewood Cliffs, N.J.: Prentice-Hall, Inc., 1970.

Set Design

James, Thurston. *The Theater Props Handbook: A Comprehensive Guide to Theater Properties, Materials, and Construction*. White Hall, Virginia: Betterway Pubs.,1987.

Pektal, Lynn. *Designing and Painting for the Theatre*. New York: Holt, Rinehart and Winston, 1975.

Thomas, Terry. *Create Your Own Stage Sets*. Englewood Cliffs, N.J.: Thames Head Ltd., Prentice-Hall, Inc., 1985.

Veaner, Daniel. *Scene Painting Tools and Techniques*. Englewood Cliffs, N.J.: A Spectrum Book, Prentice-Hall, Inc., 1984.

Lighting

Cunningham, Glen. *Stage Lighting Revealed: A Design and Execution Handbook*. Cincinnati, Ohio: Betterway Books, 1993.

Rosenthal, Jean, and Lael Wertenbaker. *The Magic of Light*. Boston: Little, Brown and Company, 1972.

History

Arnott, Peter. *The Theatre in Its Time: An Introduction*. Boston: Little, Brown and Company, 1981.

Aylesworth, Thomas G. *Broadway to Hollywood*. New York: Gallery Books, W.H. Smith Publishers, Inc., 1985.

Gottfried, Martin. *Broadway Musicals*. New York: Harry N. Abrams, 1979.

Jackson, Arthur. *The Best Musicals, from Showboat to A Chorus Line*. London: Webb and Bower, Crown Publishers, 1977.

Dance

Humphrey, Doris. *The Art of Making Dances*. New York: Grove Press, 1978.

Costume Design

Emery, Joy Spanabel. *Stage Costume Techniques*. Englewood Cliffs, N.J.: Prentice-Hall, Inc. 1981.

Jackson, Sheila. *Simple Stage Costumes and How to Make Them*. London: Studio Vista; New York: Watson-Guptill Publications, 1968–1970.

Motley. *Designing and Making Stage Costumes*. New York: Watson-Guptill Publications, 1964.

Stagecraft

Gassner, John. "Producing the Play." In *New Scene Technician's Handbook,* edited by Philip Barber. New York: Holt, Rinehart and Winston, 1953.
Lord, William H. *Stagecraft 1—A Complete Guide to Backstage Work.* Colorado Springs: Meriwether Publishing Ltd., 1991.
Sweet, Harvey. *Handbook of Scenery, Properties, and Lighting.* Vols. 1 & 2. Needham Heights, Mass.: A Longwood Professional Book; Allyn and Bacon, A Simon and Schuster Company, 1995.

Makeup

Corson, Richard. *Stage Make-up.* 8th ed. New York: Appleton-Century Crofts, 1975.

Catalogs, Brochures, Videos

Bob Kelly Cosmetics, Inc., 151 West 46th St., New York, NY 10036.
Ben Nye Makeup, 5935 Bowcroft Street, Los Angeles, CA 90016.

Selected Magazine List

American Theatre.
Theatre Communications Group
355 Lexington Avenue
New York, NY 10017
Lighting Dimensions. The Magazine for
Lighting Professionals.
P.O. Box 425
Mt. Morris, IL 61054-0425
The New York Theatrical Sourcebook.
Sourcebook Press, Inc.
163 Amsterdam Ave., #131
New York, NY 10023
Phone: (212) 496-1310

Opera News.
> The Metropolitan Opera Guild
> 70 Lincoln Center Plaza
> New York, NY 10023-6593

Showmusic. The Musical Theatre Magazine.
> Goodspeed Opera House Foundation
> Goodspeed Landing, East Haddam,
> CT 06423

Simon's Directory of Theatrical
  Materials Services & Information.
> c/o Package Publicity Services,
> Inc.
> 1564 Broadway
> New York, NY 10036

Stage Directions. The Practical Magazine of Theatre.
> P.O. Box 41202
> Raleigh, NC 27690-2930

TCI (formerly *Theatre Crafts*).
> P.O. Box 470
> Mt. Morris, IL 61054-0470

TD & T (*Theatre Design and Technology*).
> USITT
> 19 West 19th Street, Suite 5A
> New York, NY 10011-4206

Glossary

Acting area   Also known as the playing space. The area of the stage or of a specific set where the actors can perform.

Apron   The area of the stage in front of the main drape. May also be a covering over an orchestra pit.

Arena theater   Any space where the performance takes place in a centered area. In true arena, the audience sits surrounding the playing area. It may be square, round, or have aspects of the same.

Aside   An author or actor technique where the performer speaks directly to the audience. In classic melodrama it is done with the back of the hand raised to the mouth.

Audition   Appearing before directors, producers, or others in anticipation of being cast in a production. May require reading, singing, and/or dancing. Also called tryouts.

Auditorium   A structure for the assembly and seating of spectators. While used as a theatre, it may not have been specifically designed as a theatre space. Also known as the "house" where the audience sits.

Backdrop   Usually a large painted muslin or canvas cloth decorated with a scene depicting a panorama of trees, cityscape, buildings, and so on. May refer to a drape on stage or to a blue sky drop. (*See* Cyclorama.)

Backing   Scenic unit placed as a wall beyond a door opening, closet, etc. May refer to money raised in support of a production's financing.

Backlight   Light aimed from the upstage area to delineate actor's head and shoulders. Helps sculpt the body against the background scenery.

Backstage	Any area behind the plaster line or the main drape. May indicate a shop area beyond the wing space.
Batten	Usually a metal pipe over the stage. Drapes, curtain, and scenery drops or units may be suspended from them. May derive from nineteenth-century British sailors working in theatre rigging, i.e., strips that fasten things down.
Batten coming in!	A call made from crew on the fly gallery to warn actors or crew below on stage. Appropriate answer is "Thank you," so communication is understood.
Blackout	A signal for the end of a scene, or the quick ending of a scene by the rapid dimming of the lights. Often indicated in the script by B.O. or BO. In musical revues, a short scene with an unexpected ending.
Blacks	Refers to the (usually) black stage drapes or curtains known as borders and legs.
Blocking	The diagrams of where and when actors will move, or the actual movements, action, or placement of the actor, as in "What's my blocking?"
Boards	Historical term for a stage space. "On the boards" meant to follow a professional career or to mount a show.
Book	The play script. Musicals refer to the libretto as the book, the music and lyrics as the score. Also a term that refers to scenery that may fold.
Border	A horizontally hung curtain above the stage that masks lights and sets and flies from the audience. May be scenic if painted or designed into setting.
Border lights	Overhead strips of lights running from side to side parallel to the proscenium. Most often found in school auditoriums with individual light bulbs that are colored red, blue, yellow, or green. Can be called X-rays. Older types are in metal housing or troughs.
Box set	A traditional room setting of three sides. The "fourth wall" is open to or faces the audience.

Break a leg!	Theatre superstition forbids wishing good luck directly, so the opposite intention, bad luck, really denotes a prayer to achieve the ultimate performance.
Build	As in music, when the tempo increases or the sound is louder (as in "to a crescendo"), or when the pace and action become faster, usually ending in a climax of some effect.
Call	The time set for a rehearsal. Most importantly, the signal given by the stage manager to actors in preparation for the start of performance. A "three-minute" call to places means the actors must get into place for the curtain to go up.
Callboard	Where notices for actors are posted. A bulletin board backstage with rehearsal notes and messages, usually overseen by the stage manager.
Cast	The actors selected for a play or the characters in a play.
Clear the stage!	An order to immediately get out of the acting space. Could be done to avoid danger or at the start of a new scene.
Clear, please!	Request made for actors to get out of the way of stagehands moving props or scenery.
Cold	No prior experience or rehearsal, such as an actor doing a "cold" reading.
Crash box	Any of various box devices, large or small, for making sound effects for crashes. May be as simple as a box, a piece of glass, and a hammer to hit and break the glass.
Cue	A point in the script when the stagehands will change the sets, lights, or props; the point when the orchestra conductor gives a downbeat. Also the word or line of dialogue or action that signals the next line or action.
Cue sheet	A carefully crafted list of cues for the technical crew backstage or the lighting effects and changes.

Cue-to-cue
Very important rehearsal, with full cast attending. Each moment of dialogue, action, or music that is a cue for a lighting effect, set change, or scene shift is rehearsed. In general, benefits the technical crew and stagehands. This rehearsal is conducted by the stage manager in preparation for "running" the show. Dialogue between cues is ignored by jumping from one cue to the next, or "cue-to-cue."

Curtain
An exclamation by the stage manager or the director to end a scene. If called urgently, it may be to avoid danger such as a fire.

Curtain(s)
Hanging drapery onstage. May be the main curtain or house curtain. Also, the main drape or rag.

Curtain call
Actors taking a bow at the end of a play. Some theatre superstitions say that curtain calls must never be rehearsed until final dress rehearsal. Some actors will not even rehearse a curtain call but go on "cold" on opening night.

Curtain line
Can be called the plaster line. The unmarked line indicating where the main drape will fall. Instruction to an actor, as in "Don't violate the curtain line."

Cyclorama
or Cyc
May be any large, preferably seamless, backdrop of blue or white muslin that may be lit to provide different color backgrounds.

Dark night(s)
The theatre is closed, or there are no rehearsals scheduled for the cast. With professionals, the night after the dress rehearsal is usually a "dark night."

Dim
The action or effect of the lights gradually decreasing in intensity by using any form of electrical dimmers. Also called Dim Out.

Dolly
A small platform on wheels or casters. Used to move stage pieces or equipment, lights, or cameras.

Double casting
Casting more than one actor per role or for use in singing, dancing choruses. Presumes one set of leads for first performance and another set for second, etc.

Downstage
  (DS) apron   The area towards the apron or the footlights—in the direction of the audience (opposite of Up Stage).

Dress parade   A special rehearsal or appearance by actors with stage lighting, preferably with settings in place for the express purpose of viewing costumes on each character. A dress parade ought to be held well ahead of a dress rehearsal.

Dress rehearsal   Final rehearsal before having an audience. The last rehearsal held with everything completed for the performance. Note: Not to be confused with the present-day practice of having preview performances, which may last a month, giving actors and playwrights opportunities to revise the play.

Electrician   A technician who assists with the hanging, focusing, and use of lighting instruments. May be the light control board operator.

Entr'Acte   The intermission. Shows used to have entr'acte scenes in front of the stage curtain.

Equity   Actors union. Actors Equity Association, or AEA.

Face   To stand directly in front of another actor.

Fade in,
  Fade out   The slow, or gradual dimming in or out of lights.

Flat   Any two-dimensional frame covered, and usually painted, used as part of a set. Sizes vary greatly, but a standard flat used to be a five feet tall, nine inches wide dimension; and was called a "box car" since it fit in the six foot opening of railroad cars when shows travelled.

Flies   The open space above the stage floor area where lights, drapes, and sets may be hung on battens.

Floor plan   The diagram (in scale) showing how the settings or set will fit on the stage. Also, a plan for the director to use in planning the blocking.

Fly gallery   Rarely found in secondary school stages. A fly gallery is the area, usually above, where the stage crew may operate scenery, lights, and drapes.

Followspot   The lighting instrument used to follow an actor around the stage play-
              ing space. Creates a strong beam of light that may be irised in or out.
              Symbol FF.

Fourth wall   The imaginary wall implied by the curtain line or the proscenium.

French scene A scene in the script where the number of characters remains the same.
              Entrances and exits of characters make a new French scene.

Fresnel   A type of lighting instrument, called non-focusable for comparative
              reasons, that is excellent for area light. Named for Jacques Fresnel,
              who developed the special lens for lighthouse beacons.

Full stage   Indicates as much of the area of the stage as can be used in a given setting.

Ghost light   Light bulb contained in a cage and mounted on a stand. Can be left on
or spirit light overnight or when the stage is not in use. Purpose is to prevent acci-
              dents by eliminating total darkness. Obscure history, but may have
              started with practice of having a lighted candle onstage to keep out
              "ghosts."

Give, or   Move away a bit so that the focus will be on another actor or area.
  give stage

Glow tape   Used to help actors see stairs or obstacles in the dark. Commercially
              produced luminous tape or paint.

Gobo   A small, flat metal plate inserted in a lighting instrument to produce a
              pattern or image effect.

Green room   An area set aside for actors to wait between scenes. The origin of the
              name is obscure, and lots of interesting suggestions exist.

Grip   The stagehand who assists a master carpenter in the shifting of scenery.
              In motion pictures the key grip is the master stagehand. May refer to a
              master electrician.

Ground row   Any low scenic unit, such as a cutout city skyline or trees, seen in pro-
              file. Used to mask lighting (from the floor) on a backdrop.

Ham	An actor who overplays his role. Deliberately attempting to upstage someone, as in "ham it up."
Heads up!	Warning call from fly gallery to tell of falling scenery, lights, batten, or tools. Followed by "Batten coming in!" indicates a runaway pipe.
Hold book	To prompt. Someone who cues lines, watches action, and makes notes of cues to assist the director.
House	The area where the audience sits. Also the size of the audience by number, as in "How's the house?"
Key light	The principal illumination that will set the tone of the lighting by its source and color.
Kill that	To stop a sequence or take a piece of scenery or prop offstage. To turn off a light, as a follow spot.
Lead	The character who is principal in a script. There may be more than one lead. May also refer to the actor playing a role.
Leko	A focusable, ellipsoidal reflector spotlight.
Levels	Raised platforms, steps, or other areas above the actual stage floor.
Lines	The speeches, hence dialogue, of a script. (*See* Line set.)
Line set	Refers to the ropes and cables that operate a specific batten or light pipe. Line sets being used to run a show are labelled, such as "Church Drop."
Linnebach projector	Large metal, almost boxlike, structure with an intense light source. Projects prepared pictures either painted on glass or assembled from gelatin.
Load in	The scheduled move into a theatre or the act of moving the scenery, lights, and props into the stage space.
Load out	Moving out.

Mask	Provide a means for or be the means of hiding an area from the view of an audience.
Motivation	The purpose or reason that gives a character the desire to do something. Establishing motivation is a principal job of the actor and director as one.
Off book	Indicates that lines and business are learned, and cast or actor no longer needs a script in hand. Happily an actor declares, "I'm off book at last!"
Offstage	Refers to the backstage area or somewhere NOT on stage. Scripts refer to any action or sound not seen as offstage.
On stage	Within the acting area or playing space.
Orchestra	May be the ensemble of musicians in the orchestra pit or the seating area of the theatre on the same floor as the stage. The *orchos* of the Greek theatre.
Pace	The rate at which things occur in a play. Not a measure of speed or rapidity, but one of intensity.
Pit	In true theatres, a lower area in front of the apron or a place where the orchestra is situated.
Places, everybody!	A cue given by the stage manager directly, or over an address system, to all personnel, cast, and crew to be in position to start the performance or rehearsal. A mandatory command given at three minutes before curtain. Also, "Places! Please!"
Plot	Light plot, costume plot, property plot, sound plot. A diagram pertinent to a function that details how a production will work.
Practical	Something that fulfills its function, as a window or door that opens versus a faux painting of a door.
Principals	The leading characters in the play.
Producer	The individual (or the organization) who provides the means for a production to happen or to be mounted. The producer may be a backer (gets money, or has it) or a theater professional who "owns" a property (a play).

Prompt book, Prompt script	The detailed action of the production in the hands of the stage man ager. Prepared by the director.
Properties, props	The personal and set pieces necessary to the "business" of the play. Pictures and lamps are set props; handkerchiefs, handbags, and canes are personal.
Property table (Prop table)	An offstage table where props are placed for the actor to pick up and where they are to be returned. Props are usually drawn or out-lined on the table for easy recognition and access and to clue a missing item.
Proscenium	The frame surrounding the stage. The audience sees the play through the proscenium opening, or arch. Could be implied if not actual.
Put in	Also referred to as a load in.
Raked stage	The angle of the stage set to conform to sightlines of outermost seats. A "raked set" may have false perspective built in or painted on it.
Ramps	Inclined planes as in "ramp and level" set.
Read-through	A rehearsal where the script is read aloud without action.
Reprise	In musicals, the repetition of a musical number or a part of one, pre-viously heard.
Run	The number of performances planned, or the length of time or seasons, a production is given.
SAG	Screen Actors Guild, a film union.
Scrim	Known as theatrical gauze, or bobbinet material. A scrim is a woven backdrop that may be viewed as transparent with light behind it or opaque when lit from front.

Set piece	A scene piece able to stand up by itself. May be a small book unit or wagon set piece.
Sides	Manuscript sides contain only the lines to be spoken by characters preceded by three or four cue words.
Sight lines	Imaginary line drawn from outermost seats through proscenium edge; indicates what audiences may be able to see.
Skydrop	Any white- or blue-colored drop to suggest sky background. May be lighted with blue gel or painted blue.
S.R.O.	Standing Room Only. Indicates a soldout production. No seating.
Stage center	Exact center of the playing area. May be UC, C, or DC.
Stage directions	Script indications for movement or action.
Stage left	When facing the audience, this is the stage area to the left side of the actor. May be divided and designated as SL, UL, DL, DSL, etc.
Stage right	Facing DS, the stage area to the actor's right side. May be divided and designated SR, UR, DR, DR, etc.
Stand by	Warning to be ready to meet a cue.
Standby	Understudy actor.
Strike! or Strike that!	To take away a set or prop. One "strikes" a show after closing night.
Tab	Usually a piece of scenic curtain painted to act as a leg.
Take it out	To raise a piece of scenery or drop on a batten.
Take stage	To move into the most dominant position on stage. Other actors are given less focus.

Teaser | A decorative or curtain border just behind the main drape. Often used as a part of a false proscenium effect.

Technical director | Crew member responsible for overseeing the construction and completion of scenery, costumes, and lights within a designated time.

Tech rehearsal | Precedes dress rehearsal for the purpose of integrating all set changes, lighting effects, costume changes, and other mechanical aspects of the show. At least one tech should be held with full cast in "performance." (*See also* Cue-to-Cue.)

Thrust stage | May be the apron area or covered orchestra pit. Any stage space that extends into the audience.

Tormentor | Vertical units (may be curtains or flats) just upstage of the proscenium arch for purpose of masking.

Traveler | Usually an upstage curtain, but one that opens from center to sides.

Trim | Setting drops, scenic pieces, legs, or borders to hang at a specific point in height or at the floor.

Trip | To make a drop or piece of scenery fold in some manner able to accommodate space or height. "Tripping" a drop usually means folding it in half before flying.

Typecasting | Casting a role because an actor naturally behaves the same as the character in the play.

Upstage | Area away from the audience or front of stage. An actor "upstages" by moving into this area, thus forcing other actors to turn their backs on the audience.

USITT | United States Institute of Theatre Technology. Members get its magazine each month.

Walk-through | A special rehearsal when actors simply walk through their stage actions without dialogue. May be held to rehearse blocking or for a dress parade.

Wardrobe	All costumes and accessories for a play. Also a storage room.
Wardrobe person	In charge of the costumes and their maintenance.
Warn (Warning)	Signal that a cue is imminent, generally within one minute.
Work light	Non-dimming lights used during rehearsals and work sessions.
Wood- shedding	A term for studying your role and learning your lines alone. Maybe stems from the days when a misbehaving child was sent to the wood-shed to think things over.

Index

About the Authors

ROBERT M. BOLAND was honored for his twenty-seven years as professor and chairman of the Fine Arts program at Berkshire Community College, Pittsfield, Massachusetts, with the dedication of The Robert Boland Theatre.

Director of more than ninety musicals, ranging from Gilbert and Sullivan to Sondheim, in schools and community theatres, he has designed more than 175 productions and choreographed 50. Mr. Boland has staged all types of productions in churches, ballparks, a stadium, a double basketball court, and all sizes and types of theatres, including an outdoor Pops concert.

In addition to teaching and directing since he received his MFA from Boston University, he has designed for the University of Massachusetts, the Albany/Berkshire Ballet, and Williams College. He has directed for Tracy Music Library in Boston.

The author of the book and lyrics of a musical presented at the University of Massachusetts, he has designed a number of productions for Mt. Greylock Regional High School, Williamstown, Massachusetts. Mr. Boland lectures on music theatre and design at Pittsfield High School, among other schools.

A director of community theatre for the Town Players of Pittsfield, he has served on the Board of Directors of the Pittsfield Community Music School, the Berkshire Playhouse, and Jacob's Pillow Dance Festival. He currently serves on the board of the Albany/Berkshire Ballet and the Berkshire Museum and as chairman of the Pittsfield Historical Commission. An experienced restorer of paintings and art works, Mr. Boland donated 160 hours of restoration to the Edith Wharton Restoration.

He studied with Dr. Doric Alviani, Sarah Caldwell, David ffolkes, Horace Armistead, Raymond Sovey, and David Pressman.

He resides in the heart of Pittsfield, in the Berkshire Hills of western Massachusetts.

PAUL ARGENTINI is a playwright, novelist, screenwriter, quondam director and actor, and freelance writer.

He's had a showcase of his play *King's Mate* at the Cubiculo Theatre in New York and has had a number of his plays performed, including *No Gas for Nick* (which he also directed) and *Pearl Seed.* Awarded a Playwriting Fellowship by the Massachusetts Artist's Foundation, he was named finalist twice and fiction finalist.

A fly fisherman and instructor, he has just completed a beginner's book for anglers, *Fly-Fishing for Fouzles* with entomylogical illustrations by Vera Argentini. His seascape paintings and sculptures are in private and corporate collections.

A former Boston and Washington, D.C., editor, reporter, and photographer, he is host of the television show "Paolo's Kitchen." A cabinetmaker specializing in Queen Anne, Chippendale, and Shaker reproductions, he was graduated from Boston University and has had short fiction and articles published. For several years he was a member of Bill Gibson's Playwright's Workshop at the Berkshire Theatre Festival.

He has written the book and lyrics for a musical show for which his bride, Vera, composed the music. Other productions include Lisa and Mona, their two grown daughters.

Paul and Vera reside in Great Barrington, also in the Berkshire Hills of western Massachusetts.

The authors, Bob and Paul, have been friends for more than thirty-five years. Bob has directed a number of staged readings of Paul's plays, and Paul has performed in *The Student Prince,* directed by Bob. The idea for this book came from mutual respect and admiration, the passion they both have for the theatre, and the desire to make a meaningful contribution to its literature.